Christianity and Islam
Two Paths, One Purpose

By: Daniel Meguille

Copyrights © 2025 by Daniel Meguille

All rights reserved.

Dedication

I dedicate this book to my beloved parents, the late Pastor Soyam Silas and Ndoudja Esther, for grounding me in my Christian roots and for the enduring legacy of faith they passed on to me. My heartfelt thanks go to Angel Meguille Soyam for the exceptional support and constant encouragement that helped bring this work to life. To my dear wife, Audrey Meguille Soyam, your love, patience, and strength have been a pillar throughout this journey. To my precious daughter, Victoria Meguille Soyam, and my sons, Daniel Meguille Soyam and Matthew Meguille Soyam, may this book serve as a reminder of our shared values and inspire you to walk in truth, love, and purpose. I also extend my sincere appreciation to my colleague, Anita Muca, for her support and contribution along the way.

Table of Contents

Preface 7
Threads of Origin 1
   Ancient Texts and Early Prophecies 1
   The Role of Historical Figures 7
   Intertwining Beliefs 13
Sacred Streams: The Holy Texts 20
   The Bible: A Blueprint of Christian Faith 20
   The Qur'an: The Divine Word 26
   Shared Narratives: The Overlapping Stories 32
The Garden of Cultural Influences 39
   Art as a Mirror of Faith 39
   Philosophical Exchanges 44
   Festivals and Traditions 50
Navigating Divergence: Key Beliefs 56
   The Nature of God 56
   Salvation and the Afterlife 62
   Role of Scriptures in Daily Life 66
The Mystical Winds of Faith and Practice 75
   Rituals of Worship 75
   The Role of Spirituality 83
   The Practice of Charity 88

Faith in Dialogue: A Timeless Exchange 95
    Historical Interactions and Exchanges 95
    Conversations of Faith 100
    The Role of Community Engagement 107

Modern Reflections: The State of Faith Today 115
    Challenges of Misunderstanding 115
    Contemporary Connections 122
    The Youth's Role 129

Visions for Unity: Pathways to Peace 138
    Fostering Dialogue 138
    The Importance of Education 144
    Building a Common Future 151

Voices of the Faithful 157
    Personal Journeys 157
    Common Struggles 166
    Stories of Reconciliation 171

In Closing: One Humanity, Many Threads 178
    Reflections on Our Shared Journey 178
    A Call to Unity 182

Daniel Meguille – Author Biography 189

Preface

In a world often defined by division, misunderstanding, and religious tension, exploring the shared values that unite us is more vital than ever. Christianity and Islam, two of the world's largest faith traditions, are frequently portrayed in contrast; yet, at their core, both strive to guide humanity toward a life of purpose, justice, and compassion under the sovereignty of one God.

This work, **"Christianity and Islam: Two Paths, One Purpose,"** does not seek to erase theological distinctions. Instead, it respects them while drawing attention to the profound moral and spiritual common ground shared by both traditions. In this spirit of dialogue—not debate, of learning—not lecturing, we examine the stories, principles, and prophets revered by Christians and Muslims alike: Abraham, Moses, and Mary.

Through this exploration, we aim to foster mutual understanding, challenge assumptions, and cultivate a sense of unity that respects individual differences and values diversity, Whether we walk the path of the cross or the path of the crescent, we are ultimately called toward the same divine purpose: to know God, serve humanity, and cultivate peace.

This preface is offered in the spirit of bridge-building—for students, seekers, and believers alike—so that, in knowing one another better, we might better reflect the compassion and wisdom of the faiths we hold dear.

Daniel Meguille BSc, FMAAT, IIA, IQA

Author

Threads of Origin

Ancient Texts and Early Prophecies

In the cradle of civilisation, ancient Mesopotamia ignited the flickering flame of spirituality that would eventually evolve into the grand tapestries of both Christianity and Islam. This subchapter embarks on a journey through the earliest texts and prophecies, gently unravelling the complex threads that bind these two great religions to their shared origins.

The Sumerians, Akkadians, Babylonians, and Assyrians were the architects of some of the earliest recorded mythology and religious thought. With their intricate pantheons comprising gods and goddesses who governed every aspect of life, they laid the groundwork for later monotheistic ideas. Temples, ziggurats, and sacred texts from this era resonate with stories that reflect profound existential questions and moral dilemmas, providing a rich foundation for the subsequent faiths.

The Epic of Gilgamesh is one of the most significant literary and spiritual artefacts from Mesopotamia. In its tapestry of adventure, the quest for immortality, and the search for divine truth, we encounter a reflection of humanity's deepest aspirations and fears. Gilgamesh, the semi-divine king of Uruk, embarks on a journey not merely for glory but prompted by the death of his close friend, Enkidu. This profound theme of friendship and the contemplation of mortality hints at the early threads of spiritual inquiry that would permeate future religious thought.

As humanity turned its gaze upward, the emergence of monotheism—a pivotal shift that underscored the role of a singular divine entity—became apparent. Amongst the multitude of deities, the figure of Abraham emerges as a beacon of monotheism. Revered as the father of faith in both Christianity and Islam, Abraham's journey profoundly resonates with the ethos of these two religions. His story, detailed in the Hebrew Bible in **Genesis 12:1-3**, is that of Abram, whom God calls to leave his homeland and promises to make him a great nation. "Now the LORD said to Abram, 'Go from your country and your kindred and your father's house to the land I will show you. " I will make of you a great nation...'" and later revered in the Qur'an, **Surah Al-An'ām** (6:74-83), Abraham questions his father Azar and his people about idol worship. He reflects on the stars, the moon, and the sun, but rejects them all as deities. 6:79 – "Indeed, I have turned my face toward He who created the heavens and the earth, inclining toward truth, and I am not of those who associate others with Allah encapsulates a narrative of obedience, sacrifice, and the covenant with God that would set the stage for future generations.

In the biblical tradition, God calls Abraham to leave his homeland and embark on a journey into the unknown. This call symbolises a physical migration and a spiritual quest, a movement from polytheism towards the unambiguous worship of one God. Abraham's sacrifices along his journey, notably the test of faith involving the eventual near-sacrifice of his son Isaac, resonate throughout the scriptures and are echoed in the Islamic tradition where the son, Isma'il, occupies a similar narrative arc.

The Historian, a constant observer of these ancient landscapes, reflects on how Abraham's trials became emblematic of humanity's struggle to define faith in the face of uncertainty. "When one stands in the ruins of ancient Ur, the dust settling upon the stones seems to whisper stories of sacrifice and devotion," they might muse. "One can almost hear Abraham's footsteps striding towards his destiny, propelled by an unyielding faith in the divine promise."

Abraham's legacy did not end with his own story; it reverberated through centuries, shaping the doctrines of his descendants. In Judaism, he is celebrated as the patriarch, the covenant bearer through whom the promise of land and prosperity is extended to the Hebrew people. Christianity inherits this narrative, presenting Abraham as a model of faith who believed in God's promises—a precursor to the coming of Christ. For Muslims, Abraham (Ibrahim) is revered as a prophet and messenger who exemplified absolute submission to Allah, a fundamental concept in Islam. **Surah Al-Baqarah (2:124-141)** describes Abraham as a leader of humanity, a builder of the Ka'ba alongside Ishmael, and a role model in faith and submission. **2:131** – "When his Lord said to him, 'Submit!' He said, 'I have submitted [in Islam] to the Lord of the worlds.'", **2:135** – "They say, 'Be Jews or Christians and you will be guided.' Say, 'Rather, [we follow] the religion of Abraham, inclining toward truth, and he was not of the polytheists.'"

Continuing through ancient texts, we focus on developing religious thought in the context of prophecy. Prophets are key figures who act as intermediaries between the divine and humanity. The prophetic tradition flourished in ancient Israel, where figures such as Moses and Elijah, and later, the prophetic writings of the Old Testament, solidified the understanding of a covenantal relationship with God. Moses, for example, plays a pivotal role in delivering the Israelites from bondage and imparting the Divine Law, depicted as an everlasting moral guide.

In the Qur'an, the narrative adopts a complementary approach by acknowledging Jesus and his pivotal role in Christian belief while incorporating the teachings of Muhammad as the final prophet.

Surah Al-Imran (3:45–55), this passage gives the glad tidings of Jesus' birth, describes his miracles, and affirms his prophet hood, **3:45** – "[Mention] when the angels said, 'O Mary, indeed Allah gives you good tidings of a word from Him, whose name will be the Messiah, Jesus, the son of Mary…'", **3:49** – "And [make him] a messenger to the Children of Israel [who will say], 'Indeed I have come to you with a sign from your Lord…'"This seamless integration reflects a thread woven across cultures and epochs, aligning the narratives of Jesus, a prophet of love and redemption, with the continuous story of prophetic revelation leading up to Muhammad. This interconnection fosters an appreciation for the divine guidance that followers of both faiths seek.

As we explore ancient texts more deeply, the impact of cultural influences cannot be ignored. The Fertile Crescent served as a melting pot of ideas, where the Babylonian exile not only led to a re-evaluation of identity but also paved the way for the integration of new thoughts and practices. The transfer of ideas from Israel to various empires, such as Babylon and Persia, created a complex dialogue that enriched sacred writings and contributed to the development of more nuanced theological frameworks in Judaism, Christianity, and Islam.

The Historian reflects on this convergence: "The ancient libraries of Alexandria were but a dream. Yet, they housed every thought possible, from the mystical to the mundane. The evolution and interconnection of prophetic thoughts suggest an interwoven destiny. Each scholar, each faithful scribe, contributed to an intellectual sanctum where ideas converged, collided, and coalesced into enduring faiths."

This exploration of ancient texts culminates in examining how the early followers of these faiths perceived prophecy. Prophecy provided a divinely orchestrated blueprint for the faithful, guiding individuals toward ethical behaviour and communal responsibility. The prophetic literature emerged as a means of expressing hope in times of despair and a call to justice in moments of societal upheaval. In both Christianity and Islam, the shared emphasis on love, community, and justice echoes through the prophets' voices, prompting believers to extend kindness and compassion to their neighbours, regardless of differing backgrounds.

As these sacred narratives evolved into their respective canonical texts, Christianity and Islam built upon the ancient foundations laid by their ancestors. The holy scriptures became not merely historical records but living texts, dynamic and applicable to the spiritual journeys of individuals across time and geography.

The Bible, as it developed, tells the story of humanity's relationship with God. Through its various literary forms—historical accounts, poetry, proverbs, and prophecy—it invites readers into a deeper understanding of divine grace, redemption, and moral living. From the illuminating Psalms to the prophetic voices of Isaiah and Jeremiah, the scripture asserts the importance of faith and justice. These themes collectively resonate within the traditions of the Christian faith.

The Qur'an similarly draws on these ancient narratives, compelling its followers to reflect on the divine miracles of history and the significance of prophecy. Surahs that recount stories of past prophets serve not merely as historical documentation but as moral parables aiming to evoke reflection and activate faith within the reader's heart. Such narratives remind followers that prophecies can evolve, adapt, and continue to guide humanity towards righteousness.

Christianity and Islam - Two paths, One Purpose

As we move into later periods, it becomes essential to recognise the continuity between ancient Mesopotamian narratives and the ever-deepening understandings of spirituality and morality that Christianity and Islam would herald. Scribes meticulously penning down their sacred texts were not simply chroniclers of divine inspiration; they engaged in dialogues with the past, revisiting stories of resilience and faith with an eye towards the future.

The ancient texts of Mesopotamia create a lineage of thought that extends beyond mere religious observance, encapsulating humanity's journey in search of meaning, belonging, and a connection to the divine. The roots of monotheism, established in epochs long past, urge us to confront the persistent questions of existence and purpose that continue to resound in the hearts of believers today.

As the Historian ponders this enduring lineage, they note, "Each sacred text is akin to a genetic thread, passed down through generations, carrying wisdom, hopes, and the indomitable spirit of seeking truth. The ancient reflections echo through time and remain relevant to the tapestries we weave in our faith journeys."

In this quest to explore the early prophecies and sacred texts, the intertwined legacies of Christianity and Islam come into sharper focus. They are more than isolated narratives; they are threads of a broader mosaic spanning cultures and understandings, shaped by ancient beliefs yet pulsating with contemporary relevance.

The journey into the heart of ancient texts and prophecies ultimately invites readers to reflect on their spiritual paths. It underscores the importance of understanding our collective history—the shared struggles, aspirations, and transcendent quests for meaning that knit us together as one humanity navigating the realms of faith.

As we explore the roots of these two great religions, it becomes clear that while we might diverge in certain doctrines and practices, faith narratives emerge from a deeply interwoven history, echoing with lessons that reverberate through time. In recognising this rich heritage, we open ourselves to the possibilities for dialogue, understanding, and peace that may bridge the gaps between us.

Thus, as we leave the ancient currents of Mesopotamian thought, we do so with a new awareness: the seeds of compassion, justice, and faith have been planted through the stories of Abraham and other pivotal figures in our shared past. These ancient legacies are not mere relics of history but vibrant resources that continue to shape the spiritual lives of millions, guiding them toward an interconnected future rooted in understanding and mutual respect.

The Role of Historical Figures

In the annals of religious history, few figures stand as prominently as Jesus and Muhammad, two eminent personalities whose lives and teachings have shaped the spiritual landscapes of billions across the globe. Their profound impact on Christianity and Islam, respectively, offers fertile ground for exploring the complexities of their messages, the historical contexts that framed their journeys, and the enduring legacies they left behind. We unearth a tapestry of faith woven through communities, cultures, and centuries by delving into the teachings, anecdotes, and interpretations surrounding these pivotal characters.

To fully grasp the significance of Jesus and Muhammad, we must first understand the environments in which they lived and the historical nuances underpinning their teachings. Jesus, born into a Jewish family around **4 B.C.E.**, grew up in a region marked by

Roman occupation and a complex socio-political landscape. His ministry unfolded amidst a backdrop of Jewish traditions intertwined with Hellenistic influences, setting the stage for his revolutionary messages. Where traditional Jewish laws focused on ritual purity and adherence, Jesus emphasised love, compassion, and inclusivity, often challenging the societal norms of his time.

His parables, simple yet profound, conveyed deep spiritual truths. The story of the Good Samaritan, for instance, transcends cultural boundaries, inviting followers to extend compassion beyond societal prejudices. This teaching echoed his core message of love for one's neighbour, which laid the cornerstone of Christian ethical teachings. When Jesus declared, "Love your enemies and pray for those who persecute you," he radicalised the understanding of love, moving it beyond familial and communal loyalty to encompass even those considered adversaries. These counter-cultural ideas laid the groundwork for a transformative movement that would later flourish into Christianity.

In contrast, Muhammad's life story began in the early 7th century in the Arabian Peninsula, a region deeply rooted in tribal affiliations and polytheistic traditions. Orphaned at a young age, Muhammad grew up in Mecca, where he gained a reputation for his integrity and wisdom, earning the title "Al-Amin," meaning the trustworthy one. As the socio-political climate in Arabia was rife with inequality and conflict, Muhammad's encounters with social injustice became a driving force behind his prophetic mission.

At the age of 40, Muhammad began receiving revelations from Allah, relayed through the Angel Gabriel, **Surah Al-Alaq (Chapter 96), Verses 1–5.** This is widely accepted as the first revelation received by the Prophet at the age of 40:

"Recite in the name of your Lord who created man from a clinging substance. Recite, and your Lord is the most Generous –Who taught by the pen –Taught man that which he knew not."

These revelations culminated in the Qur'an, a text that brought forth a comprehensive guide for personal conduct, societal ethics, and communal governance. Central to Muhammad's teachings was monotheism, the concept of the oneness of God, which called for a radical shift from the idolatrous practices prevalent in society at the time. The declaration of faith, "La ilaha illallah, Muhammadur rasulullah" (There is no god but Allah, and Muhammad is the Messenger of Allah), became the foundational tenet of Islam, unifying a fractured society under the principles of justice and moral rectitude.

As both figures emerged in contrasting societies, their messages addressed pressing issues of their times, resonating deeply with their followers. Jesus encouraged an internalised form of righteousness, teaching his followers to cultivate a personal relationship with God through faith and grace. On the other hand, Muhammad established a framework that included personal piety and communal responsibility, integrating spirituality with social justice. The contrasting emphases in their teachings reveal how both figures responded to the unique challenges in their respective historical contexts.

Despite their differing approaches, significant similarities exist in their underlying messages. Jesus and Muhammad preached compassion, emphasising the importance of caring for the poor and marginalised. In **Matthew 5:1-7:29,** Jesus' Sermon on the Mount, which includes the Beatitudes, extols the virtues of humility and mercy. Similarly, the concept of Zakat in Islam, **Surah Al-Baqarah, 2:43,** *"And establish prayer and give zakah and bow*

with those who bow [in worship and obedience]," mandates charitable giving, underscoring the financial responsibility towards those in need. This shared value system illustrates their roles as moral compasses in their societies and highlights the intertwined nature of their messages amidst cultural diversity.

Their teachings also established more than just spiritual principles; they set the stage for communal identities that would define the followers of Christianity and Islam for centuries. Both religions, emerging from a common Abrahamic tradition, adapted their founders' teachings to reflect their respective communities' evolving cultural and social landscapes., For example, the early Christian community, as depicted in the Acts of the Apostles, **in Acts 2:44-45 (NIV),** *"**All the believers were together and had everything in common. They sold property and possessions to give to anyone who had need.**"* reflected unique practices that centred not only on the teachings of Jesus but also on the palpable experience of being part of a divine narrative. This community emphasised shared meals, prayer, and fellowship, laying the groundwork for Christian liturgical practices that persist today.

Conversely, as Islam developed after Muhammad's revelations, the ummah or community of believers emerged as a salient concept. **Surah Al-Ahzab (33:6):** *"**The Prophet is more worthy of the believers than themselves...**"* Muhammad not only functioned as a spiritual leader but also as a political figure, establishing the Medina covenant to ensure cooperation among various tribes, the Qur'an does not explicitly mention the Constitution (or Covenant) of Medina by name, but it supports and reflects the Prophet Muhammad's role as both spiritual and political leader, particularly during the Medina period, where he governed a multi-tribal, multi-religious society. This holistic approach unified followers under shared beliefs and practices, fostering an evolved sense of identity. The emphasis on community in Islam remains integral, with practices such as congregational prayers and communal fasting during Ramadan reinforcing the collective nature of faith and a sense of belonging.

As we examine the impact of Jesus' and Muhammad's teachings throughout history, it becomes clear how their lives have inspired countless generations. Anecdotes from the lives of their followers emphasise the continued relevance of their messages. For instance, the story of **Saint Francis of Assisi (1181/82–1226)** embodies the essence of Jesus' teachings on simplicity and compassion. Renouncing wealth, he embraced a life of poverty, treating all living beings with kindness. His connection with nature, evident in his patronage of animals, speaks to the universal values of reverence and stewardship that echo the ecological elements within both religions.

Similarly, figures like Rumi **(1207–1273)** in the Islamic tradition exemplify how Muhammad's influence has spurred a rich tradition of poetry and mystical expression. Rumi's works often reflect thematic connections between the individual and the divine, resonating with the profound love for God prevalent in Islamic mysticism and Christian spirituality. His poetry exemplifies how the essence of Muhammad's teachings can inspire creativity and introspection, facilitating a deeper understanding of the divine in diverse ways.

Across different cultures, the figures of Jesus and Muhammad have transcended their historical contexts to embody ideals of justice, mercy, and love. In contemporary society, movements inspired by their teachings advocate for peace and reconciliation in conflict-ridden regions. For example, interfaith dialogues facilitated by various organisations often draw upon shared values articulated by both leaders, fostering connections that transcend religious divides. Initiatives where Christians and Muslims engage in service projects illuminate the possibilities for cooperation and mutual respect, evoking the spirit of unity that both figures heralded in their lifetimes.

As we examine their historical legacies, it is crucial to reflect on the diverse interpretations that their teachings have inspired over time. The New Testament and the Qur'an, although originating from similar theological beginnings, have undergone various readings and adaptations in response to the cultural and political climates of their respective eras and the times of persecution faced by Jesus' early followers differed from the socio-political pressures experienced by Muhammad and his companions, shaping the trajectories of Christianity and Islam in distinct ways.

For instance, early Christian communities in the Roman Empire often faced disdain and violence, leading to a theology that focused on suffering and martyrdom. In **Acts 5:40-41**: "They called the apostles in and had them flogged. Then they ordered them not to speak in the name of Jesus and let them go. The apostles left the Sanhedrin, rejoicing because they had been counted worthy of suffering disgrace for the Name."

In contrast, after Muhammad's teachings gained a foothold in Arabia, the narrative shifted towards communal resilience and social justice, as the newly unified Muslim community sought to assert its identity in a landscape fraught with tribal conflicts, **Surah Aal Imran (3:103)**: *"And hold firmly to the rope of Allah all together and do not become divided..."*

Concurrently, the emergence of sects within both faiths further complicates the understanding of Jesus and Muhammad's roles. The differences between Sunni and Shia Islam and the numerous denominations within Christianity illustrate how the interpretations of these faiths' teachings have led to diverse expressions of faith. The debate around theological points often overshadows the foundational messages, prompting reflections on how sectarian divides can obscure the shared roots of love and compassion ingrained in their teachings.

In closing, the legacies of Jesus and Muhammad are not monuments confined to historical texts; they are vibrant, living truths that continue to inspire faith, challenge injustice, and cultivate hope worldwide. As followers of both religions reflect on their teachings, they hold a mirror to their lives, inviting examination, empathy, and unity. The powerful narratives surrounding these two historical figures remind us that amidst the complexities of our shared history, the essence of humanity rests in the very principles they embodied: love, justice, and mercy, which transcend religious boundaries and ignite the timeless call for peace and understanding in a diverse world.

Intertwining Beliefs

Few narratives in the landscape of world religions are as compelling as the intertwined beliefs of Christianity and Islam. At the heart of both faiths lies a rich tapestry woven from threads of shared values, traditions, and experiences. This subchapter will explore the profound concepts of faith, mercy, and community that form the foundation of Christianity and Islam, revealing how these intertwined beliefs have evolved and continue to shape millions worldwide.

Christianity and Islam - Two paths, One Purpose

Faith, in its most fundamental sense, is the unwavering certainty in the unseen. The spark ignites the soul's desire for connection with the Divine. Christians and Muslims believe in God's existence, perceiving Him through distinctive yet complementary lenses. For Christians, faith is characterised by a personal relationship with Jesus Christ, whom they believe is the incarnate Son of God. By contrast, Muslims view faith as surrendering to the oneness of Allah (God), whose teachings were revealed through the Prophet Muhammad.

In both traditions, the nature of faith encourages followers to seek a deeper understanding of their spirituality. This quest is not just personal but also communal. Faith is often expressed together in Christian churches during worship, where hymns and prayers promote unity. Similarly, in Islam, congregational prayers during Jummah (Friday prayer) build a sense of brotherhood and sisterhood, bringing Muslims together in worship and shared belief.

The concept of mercy serves as another powerful link between Christianity and Islam. Both faiths teach that mercy is an essential attribute of God, one that believers are called to emulate on a daily basis. In Christianity, God's mercy manifests in the teachings of Jesus, who spoke of love and forgiveness. Notably, the Sermon on the Mount emphasises the importance of showing mercy to others, illustrating a compassionate approach to relationships that can lead to reconciliation and healing.

Conversely, mercy is a central theme in the Qur'an, particularly in its opening chapter, **Surah Al-Fatiha (1:1–3):** *"In the name of Allah, the Most Gracious, the Most Merciful. Praise be to Allah, the Lord of the worlds. The Most Gracious, the Most Merciful,"* which proclaims Allah as the Most Merciful and the Most Compassionate. This introductory invocation lays the foundation for

Islamic teachings, which emphasise that followers should aspire to embody these attributes in their interactions with others. Both faiths encourage their adherents to practice mercy in words and through actions, urging individuals to reach out to those in need and extend forgiveness to one another.

Community is the third thread that weaves together Christian and Islamic beliefs. Both religions recognise the importance of belonging to a larger familial and spiritual network. In Christianity, the concept of the Church as the Body of Christ emphasises the importance of believers supporting one another. This communal aspect is enhanced through baptism, communion, and various ceremonies that celebrate life's milestones together. **Romans 12:4–5 (NIV):** *"For just as each of us has one body with many members, and these members do not all have the same function, so in Christ we, though many, form one body, and each member belongs to all the others."*

Islam also emphasises community through the concept of Ummah, which denotes the collective body of Muslims worldwide. It serves as a reminder that individuals are part of a global family, bound by their shared faith in Allah and the teachings of Muhammad. Festivals like Eid al-Fitr and Eid al-Adha further reinforce this sense of belonging and collective celebration, bringing families and communities together in joyous observance. **Surah Al-Mu'minun (23:52):** *"Indeed this, your Ummah, is one Ummah, and I am your Lord, so fear Me.*

As we delve deeper into the intertwined beliefs of Christianity and Islam, we find that these themes resonate beyond the surface level, calling for an exploration of how they have emerged and evolved throughout history. Understanding the historical development of these beliefs allows us to see that they are not static; instead, they are dynamic, shaped by the social and political contexts in which they exist.

One key historical moment that accelerated the intertwining of faith and community in both religions was the period of the early Church and the early Muslim community. The nascent Christian era saw believers facing persecution and societal alienation, which led them to form a close-knit community. Acts of the Apostles demonstrates this early commitment to shared property, faith, and mutual support, emphasising the importance of community as a fundamental aspect of Christian identity.

Similarly, the early Muslim community in Medina, formed after the Hijrat (migration) from Mecca, exemplified the interplay of faith and community. Here, the migration marked a geographical shift and a significant development in collective identity as Muslims established social contracts, governance, and communal prayers, which further solidified their sense of belonging and reinforced their faith. **Surah Al-Hashr (59:9–10) — On Brotherhood and Sacrifice,** *"And [also for] those who were settled in the Home (Medina) and adopted the faith before them, they love those who emigrated to them and find no hesitation in their hearts for what they have been given but give [them] preference over themselves..."*

Thus far, faith, community, and mercy intertwine in a historical narrative spanning centuries. Reflecting upon these themes within personal spiritual journeys sheds light on how individuals navigate their faith experiences while embracing the shared values in both religions. In moments of personal doubt or during life's trials, belief in a compassionate, merciful deity provides comfort and strength.

Christianity and Islam - Two paths, One Purpose

For many Christians, writing in prayer journals or participating in small group Bible studies offers both a means of personal reflection and communal engagement, allowing them to share their struggles and victories in faith. **James 5:16 (NIV):** *"Therefore, confess your sins to each other and pray for each other so that you may be healed. The prayer of a righteous person is powerful and effective."*

For Muslims, the practice of dua (supplication) serves as a means to connect personally with Allah, while also encouraging communal prayers during gatherings or events where the blessings of faith are discussed and cultivated. **Surah Al-Baqarah (2:186):** *"And when My servants ask you concerning Me – indeed I am near. I respond to the call of the supplicant when he calls upon Me. So let them respond to Me and believe in Me that they may be [rightly] guided."*

This introspective journey leads to a crucial understanding that transcends distinct religious boundaries. The shared values of faith, mercy, and community can inspire dialogue and foster relationships that promote learning and respect. It is this journey of recognition and reflection, this quest for understanding, that empowers individuals to see their similarities and nurture connections across religious divides.

In today's ever-evolving world, where division often leads to conflict, the need for compassion remains paramount. People of faith are called to rise above differences and engage with one another respectfully, recognising that their intertwined beliefs can serve as a foundation for coexistence. Through acts of kindness, whether in daily life or through organised interfaith initiatives, Christians and Muslims can manifest the mercy their faiths so passionately extol.

Christianity and Islam - Two paths, One Purpose

For instance, charitable efforts where Christians and Muslims unite to address societal issues demonstrate how shared values can lead to meaningful activism. These initiatives not only work towards alleviating social problems but also allow individuals from both faiths to engage in shared experiences, discovering anew the richness of their intertwined beliefs.

Reflecting on stories shared by members of both communities reveals how acts of mercy and community involvement have transformed lives. Muslims who volunteer at church-run shelters and Christians participating in outreach programs organised by mosques showcase the potential for connection and understanding rooted in faith. These stories echo the message that our shared humanity is far more significant than the differences that often divide us.

The importance of navigating spiritual journeys together cannot be underestimated. The Discoverer's perspective here helps to highlight the clarity that arises when people from both faiths engage in genuine dialogue. In such interactions, preconceived ideas can be challenged, and stereotypes broken down, paving the way for a deeper understanding of what it means to live out one's faith in a diverse world.

As we traverse the intertwining beliefs of Christianity and Islam, we are often surprised to discover how closely aligned their core values are. This realisation can be empowering, allowing individuals to reflect on their journeys of faith while drawing inspiration from the teachings of others. By embracing these shared foundations, believers can encourage one another to embody the virtues of mercy and community.

This shared spirituality landscape fosters a deeper appreciation for interfaith dialogue and encourages open conversations about belief. It prompts adherents to ask themselves not only what divides them but also what unites them. By understanding the essence of faith as a communal experience, followers of Christianity and Islam can find opportunities for collaboration around the values they hold dear.

Moreover, focusing on the comparative study of religious texts and teachings, the next generation can be equipped to navigate the landscapes of faith with respect and awareness. Education becomes a fertile ground for planting the seeds of compassion, growth, and unity.

As the chapters of our lives continue to unfold, may we allow the intertwined beliefs of Christianity and Islam to guide us toward a shared commitment to faith, mercy, and community. Embracing these values fosters genuine connection, an opportunity to illuminate the path of collaboration and friendship in a world that often needs such light.

Ultimately, the essence of faith that transcends religious boundaries invites us to venture forth not as isolated individuals but as members of a greater community. By recognising our intertwined beliefs, we can continue to build bridges across differences, embracing our shared mission to foster understanding, compassion, and unity in all aspects of human interaction. This is the transformative power of recognising the intertwined beliefs between Christianity and Islam, a power that, when fully embraced, can chart the course toward a more harmonious world.

Sacred Streams: The Holy Texts

The Bible: A Blueprint of Christian Faith

The Bible stands as a monumental testament to faith, constituting the sacred scriptures of Christianity. Its multifaceted composition, ranging from historical narratives to poetic literature, serves as a blueprint for Christian belief and practice, illustrating the profound relationship between humanity and the divine. The structure of the Bible reveals the evolution of its teachings and the historical contexts in which they were developed, mirroring the dynamic flow of a great river that adapts to its surroundings while maintaining its essence. Through exploration of its components, key themes, and narratives, we will uncover how this sacred text reshapes lives and fosters community engagement among its followers.

The Bible is primarily divided into two parts: the Old Testament and the New Testament. The Old Testament, also revered in Judaism, is rich with laws, prophecies, poetry, and stories that span centuries. It begins with the Pentateuch, the first five books traditionally attributed to Moses, which encompass foundational narratives, including the creation of the world, the covenant with Abraham, and the Israelites' journey from slavery to freedom. The historical books that follow recount the establishment of Israel as a nation, the reigns of its kings, and the eventual exile of the people, conveying a profound sense of identity, struggle, and divine guidance.

The poetic and wisdom literature found within the Old Testament, such as Psalms and Proverbs, elevates the emotional and philosophical dimensions of faith. Here, readers encounter expressions of worship, lament, and praise that resonate deeply with the human experience. These texts remind believers of the importance of community in their spiritual journeys, illustrating that faith is both an individual and a collective pursuit. The prophetic writings, filled with calls to repentance and visions of hope, challenge the faithful to uphold justice and mercy, reflecting God's unwavering commitment to His people.

Transitioning to the New Testament, we find the fulfilment of the promises made in the Old Testament with the arrival of Jesus Christ. The four Gospels — Matthew, Mark, Luke, and John — provide distinct yet complementary portraits of Jesus' life, teachings, death, and resurrection. Each Gospel writer offers a unique perspective on the significance of Jesus' message, emphasising different aspects of His character and mission. From the Sermon on the Mount to the parables of the Good Samaritan and the Prodigal Son, these narratives shape the ethical and spiritual frameworks that guide Christian life today.

The Acts of the Apostles further chronicles the early Christian community, illustrating how the resurrection of Jesus galvanised His followers to spread the message of salvation. The apostles' preaching centred on the resurrection, and it empowered their ministry, **Acts 4:33 (NIV),** *"With great power the apostles continued to testify to the resurrection of the Lord Jesus. And God's grace was so powerfully at work in them all."* This transitional period, marked by the outpouring of the Holy Spirit, highlights the communal aspects of faith as believers navigated the complexities of a burgeoning church amidst persecution and cultural diversity. The Pauline Epistles and the general letters that follow address various issues within the early church, providing both theological insights and practical exhortations that continue to resonate with believers.

Central to the message of the Bible is the theme of love—both God's love for humanity and the call for believers to love one another. Jesus' commandment to love one's neighbour as oneself encapsulates the essence of Christian doctrine, guiding interactions within the community and beyond. **Matthew 22:37-39 (NIV),** "Jesus replied: 'Love the Lord your God with all your heart and with all your soul and with all your mind, this is the first and greatest commandment. And the second is like it: 'Love your neighbour as yourself.' "This principle is not merely theoretical; it manifests in actions both big and small. Many devout Christians find inspiration in their scriptures, leading them to engage in acts of kindness, undertake service projects, and participate in outreach programs that uplift those in need.

Throughout biblical history, the imagery of water serves as a powerful symbol of renewal, sustenance, and divine presence. Just as a river nourishes the land around it, the messages within the Bible provide sustenance for spiritual growth. In the Gospel of John, Jesus speaks of living water, inviting those who are thirsty to come and drink, promising that it will quench their most profound spiritual longings. Such imagery echoes through Christian liturgy and community life, reinforcing the idea that the Bible is not static but living and active, continually calling believers to deeper understanding and action.

As we explore key themes within the Bible, the idea of redemption emerges prominently. Each narrative within the text unveils aspects of humanity's struggle and God's unwavering grace. From the Exodus story, where Moses leads the Israelites to freedom, to the New Testament's depiction of the crucifixion and resurrection, the theme of redemption reveals God's consistent involvement in history and His desire to reconcile humanity to Himself. Followers of Christ draw upon these stories to affirm their hope and purpose, understanding that their narratives of struggle and triumph are woven into the greater tapestry of faith.

In addition to the overarching themes, the narratives within the Bible illustrate the relational nature of faith. Personal stories, such as that of Ruth and Naomi or David and Jonathan, highlight the importance of loyalty, love, and community support. These accounts resonate with readers who may experience similar dynamics in their own lives, reminding them that faith is nurtured within relationships that reflect God's love. The presence of such relatable characters empowers believers to embrace vulnerability and forge deeper connections with one another, thus enriching their faith journeys.

Moreover, the Bible's role in shaping the Christian community cannot be overstated. As congregants gather to study scripture, engage in worship, and share their lives, the narratives contained within the Bible serve as a foundation for building a shared identity. Church services typically centre around the reading and interpretation of scripture, creating opportunities for dialogue and reflection. The preaching and teaching of biblical texts encourage individuals to apply lessons learned to everyday situations, fostering a sense of accountability and stewardship among members.

Devout Christians often view the Bible not merely as a historical document but as a guide for living in the world today. They find in its pages teachings and principles that stimulate personal growth and communal responsibility. Many report that daily scripture readings provide solace and direction, with selected verses inspiring their actions throughout the day. The practice of meditation on biblical texts cultivates inner peace, allowing individuals to connect with God's presence amid the noise of life.

Communities fuelled by the principles found in the Bible extend their influence beyond the church walls, becoming active participants in social justice, advocacy, and environmental stewardship. Through engagement in initiatives that reflect Jesus' teachings, believers demonstrate the relevance of scripture in addressing contemporary issues. For example, food banks, clothing drives, and homelessness outreach are often driven by a biblical mandate to care for the least of these, as expressed in both the Old and New Testaments.

Furthermore, the Bible has played a pivotal role in shaping the ethical frameworks within society. From its teachings on justice, mercy, and humility to the guidance of living a life of integrity and compassion, scripture provides a resource for individuals striving to navigate moral dilemmas. Many derive their understanding of right and wrong from biblical teachings, which have influenced civil rights movements, humanitarian efforts, and community programs aimed at fostering peace and understanding.

The social implications of scripture also extend to interfaith dialogues, where biblical narratives serve as points of connection between Christians and followers of other faiths. While the Bible is a distinctly Christian text, its moral teachings resonate with the tenets of many religions, leading to collaborative initiatives that pursue social equity and shared values. In confronting issues such as poverty, discrimination, and injustice, sacred narratives become bridges rather than barriers, supporting the notion that despite differing beliefs, humanity shares a common responsibility to love and serve one another.

The Bible further invites believers to consider the future with hope. The prophetic literature, alongside the visions described in the Book of Revelation, encourages an eschatological perspective that anticipates the fulfilment of God's promises. For many Christians, hope in eternal life and the promise of God's Kingdom are vibrant motivators for action in the present. The narratives compel believers to live with intention, recognising that their choices impact both their immediate communities and the larger world.

As we reflect on the Bible as a blueprint of faith, we cannot overlook the transformative impact it has on individual lives. Personal testimonies reveal the profound ways in which scriptural teachings have altered perspectives, encouraged resilience, and fortified faith. Many believers recount pivotal moments where verses or narratives provided clarity during times of crisis, acting as a lifeline in turbulent waters. This intersection of personal experience with the collective wisdom contained in the Bible illustrates how scripture speaks to the heart, urging believers toward growth and transformation.

In summation, the Bible serves not only as a religious document but also as a living testament to the journey of faith. Its diverse structure, rich narratives, and timeless themes resonate across generations, inviting believers into a dynamic relationship with God and with one another. The imagery of a flowing river vividly captures the adaptability and relevance of these sacred texts, emphasising their ability to meet people in their context and provide guidance for all aspects of life.

As devout Christians continue to glean insights from the Bible, their engagement with its stories fosters a vibrant community rooted in shared beliefs and inspired actions. With each passage read, the scripture imparts wisdom, ignites passion, and compels individuals to reflect on their roles in building a just and compassionate world. Ultimately, the Bible stands as a guiding light, illuminating the path of faith and inspiring transformative actions in the lives of those who embrace its teachings.

The Qur'an: The Divine Word

The Qur'an stands as a monumental pillar of faith for over a billion Muslims worldwide. It is not just a text; it is considered the very word of God, revealed to the Prophet Muhammad over a period of twenty-three years. As such, the Qur'an takes on unique attributes that set it apart from other religious texts, embodying principles that resonate deeply within the lives of its adherents. In exploring the significance of the Qur'an, we delve into its structural intricacies, its profound teachings, and how it extends beyond mere recitation into the daily lives of practising Muslims.

The Qur'an is composed of 114 chapters, known as surahs, each varying in length and thematic content. From the outset, readers will notice the flow of language and the rhythmic prose that marks its verses. This stylistic quality has led many to consider the Qur'an not only a spiritual guide but also a work of literary beauty. **Surah Al-Fatiha**, for instance, is often cited as the essence of the Qur'an, encapsulating the core themes of faith, guidance, compassion, and devotion. As a daily prayer, this surah prepares the believer's heart, making it an integral part of Islamic worship.

The first verse of **Al-Fatiha** reads, **"In the name of Allah, the Most Gracious, the Most Merciful,"** emphasising the foundational attributes of God in Islam. This invocation sets the tone for understanding the relationship between Creator and creation. These attributes of mercy and compassion permeate the entire Qur'an, providing a thematic backdrop for the guidance and teachings it offers.

Moving forward, significant surahs illuminate essential principles that Muslims are encouraged to integrate into their conduct. **Surah Al-Baqarah**, the longest chapter of the Qur'an, spans several pivotal themes, including the importance of faith, the nature of community, and the essence of obedience to divine will. One of its notable verses, **Ayat Al-Kursi** (The Throne Verse), eloquently expresses God's sovereignty and omnipotence: "Allah! There is no deity except Him, the Ever-Living, the Sustainer of existence. Neither drowsiness overtakes Him nor sleep. To Him belongs whatever is in the heavens and whatever is on the earth." This verse is often recited for protection and is revered for its encapsulation of God's profound significance in the life of a believer.

Guidance is another cornerstone theme of the Qur'an, permeating many chapters and verses. **Surah Al-Anfal** emphasises the importance of community and collective morals, delineating ethical behaviour that aligns with Islamic principles. Here, verses discuss issues of justice and compassion, urging believers to act righteously not only in their conduct but also in the broader societal context. The recommendation for social justice, equity in dealings, and compassion for the less fortunate is a recurring message that resonates throughout the sacred text.

Personal narratives from practising Muslims often illustrate the profound connection they maintain with the Qur'an. A practising Muslim, Fatima, shares her experience of growing up in a household where the Qur'an was not just a book on the shelf but a living part of the family's daily ritual. "Every morning began with a recitation," she reminisces, explaining how her parents encouraged her to engage with the text, ensuring she understood its meanings and application. "The Qur'an wasn't just something we recited; it was an integral part of our lives. It shaped our values and brought a sense of peace and clarity in challenging times."

Fatima recalls a particular incident when she faced uncertainty in her life regarding her career choices. During a challenging moment, she turned to **Surah Al-Baqarah**, specifically **verse 286**, which reassures believers that, *"Allah does not burden a soul beyond that it can bear."* This wisdom from the Qur'an helped her navigate her fears, reinforcing her belief in divine support and guidance.

Moreover, the Qur'an's principles of charity and compassion are illustrated beautifully in **Surah Al-Insan**. This surah makes a poignant appeal for generosity and kindness towards the less fortunate: *"And they give food, despite their hunger, to the needy, the orphan, and the captive."* Such teachings reinforce the social fabric of Muslim communities, where charity becomes not just an act of kindness but a moral obligation woven into the life of every Muslim.

The act of engaging with the Qur'an is transformative, as recounted by volunteers in community service. Ahmed, a community leader, shares how a study group interpreting **Surah Al-Ma'idah** motivated his peers to establish a food bank. "The text inspired us to act, to serve our community, and to put our faith into practice," Ahmed explains. The surah's emphasis on lawful food and mutual support illustrates how the Qur'an nurtures a sense of responsibility towards others, thus facilitating collective action for the greater good.

Beyond its verses, the Qur'an resonates in cultural expressions through art, calligraphy, and recitation. The art of Quranic calligraphy not only beautifies the text but also signifies its sacredness, often seen in mosques and homes. These intricate designs reflect the reverence Muslims have for the words contained within the pages—a visual reminder of the divine presence in everyday life.

Additionally, the practice of reciting the Qur'an with tajweed, or the rules of recitation, creates an auditory experience that enhances understanding and spiritual connection. Layla, an Arabic teacher, emphasises this point by saying, "When my students learn to recite properly, they aren't just learning a language; they are accessing an experience that connects them with their faith." This connection deepens the appreciation of the Qur'an, allowing its messages to resonate in the minds and hearts of believers long after the recitation has ended.

As Muslims engage with the Qur'an, they come to recognise the complexities of its guidance. **Surah Al-Tawbah** addresses the concept of repentance and seeking forgiveness, teaching that God's mercy is vast and accessible to all who sincerely seek it. This notion upholds an essential aspect of Islamic theology—that regardless of one's past, redemption is a possibility for anyone. Such messages foster hope and renewal, propelling individuals toward self-improvement and a continual striving for righteousness.

In contemporary society, the Qur'an remains a source of solace amid chaos. During trying times, such as natural disasters or personal crises, many Muslims reflect on the comfort offered in verses that emphasise God's presence and support. **Surah Al-Ra'd states, "Indeed, with hardship comes ease,"** which serves as a reminder that opportunities for growth and healing often accompany challenges. Such teachings encourage believers to remain steadfast, instilling resilience in the face of adversity.

Furthermore, the Qur'an instils a sense of accountability, particularly regarding social justice. The verses contained within **Surah An-Nisa** urge believers to uphold justice, calling upon them to defend the oppressed and to stand against injustice, regardless of the circumstances. This principle has sparked movements and initiatives aimed at social reform within various Muslim communities worldwide, demonstrating the Qur'an's relevance in advocating for societal betterment.

The teachings of the Qur'an are woven intricately into communal practices and social values. During Ramadan, the holy month of fasting, Muslims devote themselves to prayer, reflection, and reading the Qur'an, deepening their connection to the sacred text. Laylat al-Qadr, the Night of Decree, commemorates the moment when the Qur'an was first revealed, further highlighting the significance of this text within the life of every believer. For many, staying awake throughout the night to engage in worship and recitation of the Qur'an fosters a profound spiritual ambience that unites families and communities.

As part of maintaining a continuous relationship with the Qur'an, many Muslims memorise verses, enhancing their commitment to learning and spiritual growth. Memorisation of the Qur'an, an act known as Hifz, is not only seen as a spiritual endeavour but also as a respected achievement within the community. Once individuals complete their memorisation, they are honoured in ceremonies celebrating their dedication—a testament to the Qur'an's role as both a guide and a life companion.

Moreover, the Qur'an encourages individuals to engage in contemplation and reflection. Verses that prompt believers to observe their surroundings and learn from nature evoke a sense of wonder and responsibility towards creation. **Surah Al-Imran** illustrates this beautifully with its call to **"reflect on the creation of the heavens and the earth"** as a means of nurturing belief. This theological and philosophical approach emphasises that understanding the Qur'an is not merely a religious practice, but a holistic exploration of existence.

The role of the Qur'an extends well beyond individual piety. It acts as a foundational text that shapes the ethical framework of societies rooted in Islamic principles. Governments in Muslim-majority countries frequently reference the Qur'an in their legal frameworks and policy-making, incorporating its teachings into systems of governance. This highlights the Qur'an's enduring power and relevance, not only within spiritual domains but also within societal infrastructure.

The Qur'an represents a rich repository of wisdom, inviting believers to discover truth, beauty, and purpose. As it interweaves themes of justice, compassion, and guidance, it challenges individuals and communities to embody these principles actively. Personal stories abound of individuals transformed by their engagement with the Qur'an, attesting to its role as a beacon of hope and a source of strength. The authentic narratives of practising Muslims remind us that the Qur'an is indeed a living text—an eternal guide that shapes lives and communities across generations.

In navigating the complexities of life, the Qur'an remains a harbinger of guidance, inviting its readers into a profound relationship with the divine. The attributes of mercy and justice, as first articulated in its verses, continue to resonate in the hearts of millions, echoing the timeless message that underneath our diverse experiences lies a shared foundation of faith and humanity. Thus, the journey through the Qur'an remains a sacred and transformative endeavour, promising growth, reflection, and an unyielding connection to the divine.

Shared Narratives: The Overlapping Stories

In the rich tapestry of religious narratives woven through the biblical and Qur'anic texts, profound similarities exist that unveil a shared heritage. Both Christianity and Islam offer intertwined stories of key figures that not only illustrate the virtues prized by both faiths but also invite believers to engage in dialogues rooted in common understanding. At the forefront of this exploration are figures such as Adam, Noah, and Mary, whose narratives span centuries and civilisations, connecting the hearts and minds of followers across different cultures and histories.

The History of Adam serves as an essential starting point in this investigation into shared narratives. In both the Bible and the Qur'an, Adam is recognised as the first human being, a figure symbolising creation and the introduction of human life into the world. According to Biblical accounts, found in Genesis, God created Adam from the dust of the earth and breathed life into him, establishing a direct and intimate relationship with the Creator. The Qur'an resonates with this depiction, detailing Adam's creation from clay and God's act of bestowing life, highlighting a shared understanding of humanity's divine origins.

Throughout the narratives, both texts emphasise the significance of Adam's role as a prophet and the first recipient of God's guidance. In Christianity, Adam is often viewed through the lens of the Fall, leading to discussions on original sin and humanity's need for redemption. The Qur'an, however, presents Adam's story with a focus on forgiveness and mercy; it acknowledges human fallibility while emphasising God's compassion upon Adam's repentance.

In reflecting on Adam's narrative, the Discoverer conveys a sense of awe at how these stories mirror each other, with divergences shaping distinct theological interpretations yet pointing towards a mutual emphasis on God's mercy and human accountability. By examining Adam's story, readers can recognise how each faith's interpretation can catalyse dialogue, promoting respect and understanding despite their differences.

Moving forward, the figure of Noah stands out as another pillar of shared narratives. Both scriptures recount the events surrounding the Flood, each imbued with its unique emphasis while maintaining essential parallels. In the Bible, **Genesis 6:8–9 (NIV),** Noah is depicted as a righteous man chosen by God to build an ark, preserving a remnant of humanity and creation through a great flood that eradicated the wickedness of the world. The Qur'anic account echoes this narrative but provides additional dimensions, including Noah's steadfastness in the face of disbelief and his plea for his people to return to God. **Surah Nūḥ (71:1–2),** *"Indeed, We sent Noah to his people, [saying], 'Warn your people before there comes to them a painful punishment.'"*

One striking aspect of both accounts is the depiction of Noah's unwavering faith in the face of adversity. In the Bible, he is portrayed as a figure who stands out in a corrupt generation, demonstrating righteous character amidst overwhelming societal decline. The Qur'an further emphasises this aspect of Noah, illustrating his tireless efforts to guide his people and revealing God's call to repentance. Here, the commonalities are not confined to the events of the Flood but reach deeper into the values represented by both figures—faith, resilience, and the call to moral integrity.

The stories of Adam and Noah highlight themes of creation, re-creation, and the complexities of humanity's relationship with God. As the Discoverer reflects on these narratives, it becomes evident that the shared elements are not merely historical accounts but are layered with moral and ethical lessons aimed at guiding individuals in their spiritual journeys. They encourage believers from both traditions to engage in dialogue about their shared values, emphasising how mutual respect can grow from understanding the collective wisdom embedded in these stories.

Next, we turn to the story of Mary, a vital figure in both Christianity and Islam. Revered in Christianity as the mother of Jesus, Mary holds an esteemed position as a symbol of purity, obedience, and maternal love. **In Luke 1:26-28 (NIV),** *"The angel went to her and said, 'Greetings, you who are highly favoured! The Lord is with you.'"* The Bible recounts her miraculous conception of Jesus, underscoring her role in the narrative of salvation, as she embraces the angel's message with faith and humility. In contrast, the Qur'an honours Mary, or Maryam, as one of the most exalted women in history, celebrating her chastity and submission to God's will.

In Surah Maryam (19:17 21): *"We sent to her Our Spirit, and he appeared before her as a man... He said, 'I am only the messenger of your Lord to announce to you the gift of a pure son.'"* **And Surah Āl-Imrān (3:45):** *"[The angels said:] 'O Mary, indeed Allah gives you good tidings of a word from Him, whose name will be the Messiah, Jesus, the son of Mary...'"*, the Qur'an provides a detailed account of the Annunciation, where the angel Gabriel delivers the news of her miraculous pregnancy. This event is significant for both faiths, as it showcases themes of divine intervention, faith, and the miraculous. While the theological implications differ—Christianity views Jesus as divine, whereas Islamic texts present him as a prophet—the affection and veneration for Mary unite followers of both faiths. Her story transcends theological nuance, serving as a beacon of hope and devotion that speaks to the struggles of motherhood and belief.

In considering these overlapping narratives, the Discoverer emphasises the inherent value of shared respect. By recognising Mary's significance across both religions, individuals can appreciate her embodiment of faith and devotion without the need for theological contention. This shared narrative invites dialogue centred on mutual appreciation and understanding of diverse perspectives about revered figures.

The exploration of these stories leads to a broader understanding of other Biblical and Qur'anic figures that echo similar teachings and moral lessons. While figures such as Abraham, Moses, and Joseph resonate profoundly in both texts, their narratives carefully illustrate how shared experiences can foster understanding and respect, moving beyond the surface differences of interpretation.

Abraham, or Ibrahim, is woven deeply into both traditions' identities as the father of monotheism. He is celebrated not only for his unwavering faith in God but also for his covenant relationship, which serves as a defining element of both his faith and the faith of his followers. The account of Abraham's near-sacrifice of his son, Isaac, in the Bible, **Genesis 22:2 (NIV),** *"**Then God said, 'Take your son, your only son, whom you love—Isaac—and go to the region of Moriah. Sacrifice him there as a burnt offering on a mountain I will show you,'**"* and Ishmael in the Qur'an underscores profound themes of faith, obedience, and commitment to God's intentions. In **Sūrat al-Ṣāffāt (37:99-113),** with additional allusions in **Sūrat Ibrāhīm (14:37) and Sūrat Maryam (19:54-55).** While the son is not named in the text, classical Muslim exegesis (tafsīr) and prophetic ḥadīth overwhelmingly identify him as Ismā'īl (Ishmael) rather than Isaac.

By unravelling the parallels between these narratives, believers are encouraged to view Abraham as a symbol of faith and a champion for justice. This shared heritage provides fertile ground for dialogue, prompting discussions on the challenges and demands of faith in contemporary society. In recognising the shared narrative of Abraham, followers of both faiths can engage in conversations that emphasise commonalities rather than divisions, leading to a deeper connection rooted in faith.

Furthermore, figures like Moses/Musa, revered for his leadership and struggles, portray another commonality that transcends theological lines. Both faiths recount his story, emphasising his role as a liberator and prophet who led the Israelites from slavery and delivered divine laws. Both narratives highlight ethical imperatives, showcasing Moses' dedication to justice, compassion, and leadership in times of crisis. In this exploration, the Discoverer recognises the parallels between their roles as leaders, inviting people of faith to consider how these stories can inform their actions in modern society, particularly in advocating for justice and peace. In the Bible, Moses is called by God at the burning bush to free the Israelites from Egyptian slavery. **Exodus 3:10 (NIV):** *"So now, go. I am sending you to Pharaoh to bring my people, the Israelites out of Egypt."* In Quran: **Surah Ṭā-Hā (20:9 14):** *"Indeed, I am your Lord. So remove your sandals. Indeed, you are in the sacred valley of Ṭuwā... I have chosen you, so listen to what is revealed."*

The narratives shared between Christianity and Islam extend beyond prophetic figures, encompassing stories of community, familial relationships, and moral teachings that highlight the intrinsic values celebrated by both faiths. The pathos of the human experience, characterised by challenges, resilience, and divine grace, emerges through these traditions, fostering a rich dialogue centred on shared struggles and aspirations.

As this subchapter draws to a close, it becomes apparent that the exploration of shared narratives serves as an essential framework for constructing meaningful interfaith dialogues. The Discoverer reflects on these connections that extend beyond mere historical accounts, instead fostering a narrative that celebrates the universality of human experiences guided by faith. In identifying these overlapping stories, readers are invited to engage in a respectful exchange, recognising the importance of understanding how shared beliefs contribute to a shared humanity.

Indeed, these narratives affirm that Christianity and Islam are not merely disparate religions but are intertwined through common threads that can lead to respect, collaboration, and love across divides. The stories of Adam, Noah, and Mary, as well as reflections on other figures such as Abraham and Moses, illustrate that at the core of both faiths lies the universal urge for faith, relationship, and divine guidance.

Consequently, as one contemplates the vastness of these shared narratives, it becomes increasingly clear that they reveal pathways to dialogue, emotional connection, and existential understanding. By delving into these commonalities, followers can shape a discourse that highlights their shared values, bolstering a spirit of friendship and respect, essential in contemporary society.

As believers from both faiths reflect upon these narratives, they are not only reminded of their sacred histories but are beckoned to build upon them in fostering understanding and harmony. The rich texture of interconnected stories is not simply an academic pursuit; it is a sacred call to engage with one another, reinforcing the bridges that connect their diverse yet intertwined legacies in faith.

The Garden of Cultural Influences

Art as a Mirror of Faith

The intertwining of faith and art has served as a dramatic canvas upon which the histories of Christianity and Islam have unfolded. From the soaring cathedrals of Europe to the intricate patterns of Arabic calligraphy, art has consistently reflected spiritual beliefs and often served as a bridge connecting the sacred to the everyday. In this exploration of artistic traditions within both faiths, we unravel the threads of expression that earlier artisans and contemporary creators have used to interpret their beliefs, affirming the indispensable role of art in the religious experience.

Christianity's artistic narrative has centuries of history, originating from its roots in the ancient world. Early Christians, facing persecution, often adopted a clandestine approach to representation. Symbolism flourished in the early church; the fish (ichthys) became a deeply significant symbol, representing Jesus Christ. Yet, as Christianity gained acceptance, particularly with the Edict of Milan in 313 AD, its artistic endeavours began to flourish visibly. The imperative to communicate the divine through tangible forms became a principal task for believers.

By the time of the Byzantine Empire, Christians had established a distinctive visual language. The use of mosaics and frescoes transformed church interiors into celestial spaces. The dome of the Hagia Sophia, adorned with shimmering gold mosaics, encapsulates the Byzantines' vision of heaven meeting earth. This artistic choice symbolised not only a theological belief about the divine but also practically cultivated a meditative space for worshippers. Each shimmering tile reflected a piece of the divine, inviting the faithful into a realm where art and spirituality mingled.

As Western Europe transitioned into the Middle Ages, Gothic architecture emerged as the dominant architectural style. Cathedrals like Notre-Dame de Paris, with their grandiose spires and stained glass windows, illustrated biblical tales, educating a largely illiterate populace through vivid imagery. The intricate designs of rose windows served as symbolic representations of divine light pouring through the narratives of salvation history. Through art, the mystique of faith found a safe harbour, and the cathedrals became sanctuaries of learning and enlightenment.

Parallel to these developments in Christianity, Islamic art emerged from its profound roots, redefining the relationship between faith and artistic expression. Following the establishment of Islam in the 7th century, the faith spread across vast territories, uniting diverse cultures with rich artistic traditions. However, the core tenets of Islam influenced how religious imagery was conceived: the avoidance of idolatry led to a distinct aesthetic that emphasised calligraphy, geometric patterns, and floral motifs.

Calligraphy became the ultimate expression of devotion in Islamic art. The Arabic script, with its fluidity and elegance, transformed language into a medium of spiritual engagement. Verses from the Qur'an were meticulously crafted, with hands skilled in the art of writing conveying reverence in each stroke. From carved stone inscriptions on mosque walls to delicate manuscripts, calligraphy intertwined itself with the sacred, emphasising the spiritual significance of God's word. Mosques such as the Alhambra in Spain exhibit this rich tradition, with walls adorned with beautifully scripted verses that invite contemplation.

Geometric patterns adorned Islamic architecture, reflecting the mathematical precision that Islamic scholars admired. The repetitive motifs not only symbolised the infinite nature of Allah but also demonstrated a cosmic order, tying the material universe to the sacred. The iconic dome of the Sultan Ahmed Mosque in Istanbul, coupled with its intricate tile work, embodies the integration of architectural prowess with spiritual meaning, serving as a reminder of the harmony between faith and the cosmos.

Art history reveals the dialogues between Christianity and Islam, particularly during periods of cultural interchange. The medieval era witnessed both civilisations flourishing through intellectual exchange, particularly in Spain during Al-Andalus. Christian artists, inspired by Islamic motifs, began to incorporate geometric designs into their work, giving rise to the Mudejar style. Churches adorned with intricate tilework echoing Islamic aesthetics stand as legacies of this intercultural collaboration.

Artists from both faiths have engaged with each other's traditions, often finding common ground in shared values such as compassion, humility, and the quest for transcendence. Renowned figures such as the Persian polymath Al-Khwarizmi and Christian scholar Thomas Aquinas exemplified this synthesising spirit, using art and scholarship to bridge the chasms of cultural and religious divides. Their works illuminate how both faiths could thrive through mutual admiration and understanding, reinforcing the notion that art serves not only as a mirror to faith but as a medium for dialogue.

The Renaissance gave rise to yet another creative awakening within Christianity, under the auspices of humanism. Artists like

Christianity and Islam - Two paths, One Purpose

Michelangelo and Raphael navigated themes of divinity and humanity, illustrating biblical stories with profound emotional depth. The Sistine Chapel became the culmination of this artistic vision, depicting the creation narrative through breathtaking frescoes that challenged viewers to contemplate their relationship with the divine. Here, the boundary between the sacred and the secular dissolved, as art became a means of personal connection with God.

Meanwhile, the Islamic world continued to flourish artistically, especially during the Ottoman Empire. It was marked by an appreciation for beauty that transcended borders. The Ottomans adopted Persian influences, resulting in a vibrant tapestry of art that is represented in textiles, ceramics, and miniature paintings. The intricate patterns decorated and unified the entirety of the object, be it a simple plate or a lavishly embroidered robe, signifying the artisans' dedication to the divine in every detail.

As the centuries unfolded, modernity brought about new perspectives. In the 19th and 20th centuries, artists began to challenge established norms and grapple with their own identities. The impact of Western art movements reached Islamic regions, resulting in a distinctive blend of traditional and contemporary expressions. Artists like Shakir Ali in Pakistan infused modernity with traditional styles, while contemporary Christian artists sought to reimagine age-old symbols in the light of current realities.

In contemporary times, the role of art remains ever relevant within both faiths. Institutions and galleries worldwide exhibit the breadth of work inspired by religious fervour, reflecting not only the depth of spirituality but also the human condition. Modern artists often face the challenge of balancing tradition with innovation, seeking resolution between ancient messages and contemporary narratives.

Community engagement through art has also opened avenues for dialogue, with collaborative projects leading to collective understanding. Interfaith art initiatives enable artists from Christianity and Islam to share spaces, creating platforms for conversation about shared histories and visions for peace. Through murals, installations, and performances, the potential for unity flourishes, amplifying voices often drowned out by misunderstanding and division.

The intertwining of art and faith illustrates a tapestry woven from diverse threads, each possessing the capacity to be both a reflection of personal belief and a vehicle for cultural exchange. The dialogues sparked by these artistic expressions continue to foster greater understanding between communities, rendering art a timeless mirror of faith.

The continuous reverberations of faith through art across cultures remain a profound reminder of how shared human experiences transcend boundaries. As we reflect on the rich artistic legacies of both Christianity and Islam, it becomes evident that art serves not merely as decoration but as a vehicle through which the divine speaks, urging followers to engage compassionately with one another in an increasingly interconnected world.

Thus, we conclude that the stories told through art remain eternally inspiring, inviting us to explore more profound truths. Whether contemplating the swirls of paint on a canvas or the intricate formations of tile in a mosque, we are called to witness the guidance embedded within the strokes and symbols, leading us toward a future where the mutual appreciation of faith and creativity can illuminate paths of unity and respect across the mirrored landscapes of Christianity and Islam.

Philosophical Exchanges

The philosophical exchanges between Christianity and Islam, particularly during the Middle Ages, represent a fascinating tapestry of thought, inquiry, and mutual influence. At a time when both religions were fervently developing their theological foundations, scholars from diverse backgrounds came together, leaving behind an intellectual legacy that would shape not only their respective faiths but also the very fabric of Western philosophy. These exchanges cultivated an environment that valued dialogue and debate, fostering a shared pursuit of truth through inquiry and teaching.

One of the most prominent figures in this era of philosophical exchange was Augustine of Hippo, a North African theologian and philosopher in the early Christian Church. His works laid the groundwork for medieval Christian philosophy, blending classical Greek philosophy, particularly Platonism, with Christian doctrine. Augustine's exploration of the nature of God, the soul, and moral philosophy highlighted the relationship between faith and reason, presenting a framework that would influence both Christian and Islamic thinkers.

In his seminal work, "Confessions," Augustine delves into the nature of the individual's relationship with God and the interior life of the believer. He famously writes about the restless human heart, a theme that resonates across cultures. The contemplation of the self and its relation to a higher power is a philosophical endeavour that transcends religious boundaries. His confessions reveal a duality of faith and intellect, portraying a journey that many thousands of believers have followed throughout the centuries. This universality of experience would be echoed by many Muslim scholars who grappled with similar questions in their own theological contexts.

In contrast, centuries later, Averroes, also known as Ibn Rushd, emerged as a pivotal thinker in the Islamic Golden Age, distinguished for his commentaries on Aristotle. His works breathed new life into Aristotelian philosophy, emphasising rational inquiry and empirical observation. Understanding the world through reason was central to Averroes's thought, where philosophy and religion could coexist. He bridged the philosophical traditions of the ancients with the rich intellectual heritage of Islamic scholarship, asserting that faith and reason were not at odds but rather complementary.

Averroes's commentaries on Aristotle became a beacon for Christian scholars in Europe, particularly during the twelfth century. After the fall of the Western Roman Empire, many classical texts were preserved within the Islamic world, leading to the rise of Latin translations that would significantly influence European universities. His ideas sparked a renaissance of scholarly pursuits in Europe, influencing figures such as Thomas Aquinas and the scholastic movement—an intellectual revival rooted in Aristotelian philosophy.

The Oxford theologian Robert Grosseteste and Norman philosopher John of Salisbury were among those who absorbed Averroes's ideas and sought to reconcile them with Christian theology. The flourishing of universities during this period—such as the University of Paris or Oxford—created hubs for learning where philosophical debates often took place in academic settings. This dynamic atmosphere was one in which thinkers from diverse backgrounds engaged in spirited discourse, generating intellectual ideas that transcended geographical and religious divides.

Amid these philosophical exchanges, the interplay between reason and faith became a central theme. Augustine's assertion that "I believe to understand" invites a dialogue with Averroes, who frequently proclaimed that rational inquiry leads one closer to the divine. Both philosophers enriched theological discourse by carving out spaces for reason and faith to converge. Augustine's works often provided a foundation for understanding divine grace, human free will, and ethics, which were deeply rooted in a metaphysical framework that directed attention towards an ordered cosmos.

In contrast, Averroes emphasised the importance of understanding the natural world. He critiqued blind faith, arguing that one must engage with philosophical principles to achieve proper understanding. This was significant during a time when dogma often overshadowed intellectual pursuits. His assertion that philosophy allows individuals to perceive the divine essence in the natural world provided a strong foothold in Islamic philosophy, emphasising a cosmology that interconnected the empirical realm with the metaphysical.

The role of universities as incubators of intellectual thought is not to be understated. These institutions did not merely serve as places of learning; they became vibrant arenas for cultural exchange. Scholars, regardless of their religious affiliations, gathered to study, teach, and debate. This intermingling of ideas gave rise to a unique synthesis of knowledge, often leading to innovations that would shape the course of Western thought.

The establishment of the University of Paris in the late twelfth century marked a watershed moment in the history of education. It became a focal point for scholarly activity, drawing students and thinkers from across Europe who were eager to engage with texts from both the Latin West and the Arabic-speaking East. This dialogue fostered a climate of inquiry, as Aristotle's works, facilitated by Islamic scholars' translations and commentaries, entered the European intellectual landscape. The universities, therefore, became key conduits for philosophical exchange, embodying the spirit of collaboration and mutual respect.

In this vibrant environment, the writings of Augustine and Averroes, amongst other thinkers, proliferated. The writings of Augustine were frequently read and debated, reflecting an engagement that was expansive yet discerning. His ideas on morality, ethics, and human nature resonated through the Gothic cathedrals and lecture halls of medieval Europe, becoming the theological backbone for Christian thinkers navigating the murky waters of faith and reason.

Similarly, the influence of Averroes led to a resurgence of Aristotelian thought within the scholastic tradition, impacting theologians such as Albertus Magnus and Thomas Aquinas. Aquinas, in particular, sought to harmonise Aristotelian philosophy with Christian theology, establishing a framework that sought to understand the divine using reason. His famous "Summa Theologica" extensively engages with both Augustinian thought and Islamic philosophy, revealing the complex interplay between rational inquiry and theological discourse.

The cross-pollination of ideas was not without its challenges. The differing interpretations of faith and reason led to tensions that rippled through both academic and religious spheres. Critics of Averroes within the Islamic tradition raised concerns about the apparent threat posed by rationalism to orthodox beliefs. Similarly, the rise of scholasticism provoked debates amongst Christian circles regarding the balance between faith and reason. Nonetheless, such challenges often ignited deeper inquiry, leading to a more nuanced understanding of theological principles across both realms.

Christianity and Islam - Two paths, One Purpose

The Middle Ages witnessed debates over the nature of God, creation, and ethics that showcased how divergent theological perspectives complemented one another, despite their differences. This dialogue prompted critical examinations of issues such as free will, moral responsibility, and the relationship between God and humanity. The spaces created for philosophical discourse represented the interconnectedness of knowledge, wherein the pursuit of truth became an enterprise shared by both faiths.

As these philosophical exchanges unfolded, they set the stage for further developments in both traditions. The Renaissance, fuelled by the rediscovery of classical philosophy, would not have occurred at the same magnitude without the groundwork laid during these earlier interactions. The legacy of figures like Augustine and Averroes created an enduring dialogue that transcended centuries, shaping not only religious thought but also scientific inquiry and emerging humanistic perspectives.

In today's context, understanding the depths of these historical exchanges may provide necessary insights into the existing divides and possibilities for interfaith dialogue. By reflecting on the shared philosophical explorations and questioning prevalent assumptions about faith and reason, the foundations set in the Middle Ages can illuminate pathways toward future collaborations.

Bridging the divides forged by time, culture, and doctrine requires a commitment to engage with one another as intellectual equals in the search for understanding. Just as Augustine and Averroes utilised inquiry and reflection to explore the divine and ethical questions of their time, contemporary scholars and believers can employ similar methods to foster mutual respect and dialogue.

Diversifying educational curricula to include the perspectives of both faiths, along with their histories, philosophies, and ethical frameworks, can enrich the understanding of contemporary global issues. By embracing the legacy of scholarly exchange, modern thinkers can lay the groundwork for a constructive dialogue that transcends differences, providing future generations with tools to navigate a complex world.

The Garden of Cultural Influences is enriched by understanding that philosophical dialogue does not merely bridge gaps; it cultivates depth, nuance, and a shared pursuit of enlightenment. The works of Augustine and Averroes urge us to reconsider our own perspectives, inviting us to engage with a multifaceted world where unity is rooted in the richness of diversity. This exploration requires not only intellectual curiosity but a commitment to honouring the threads that bind humanity together, encouraging the continual weaving of shared narratives.

In light of this exploration, the philosophical exchanges between Christianity and Islam underscore a crucial lesson for our time: the importance of dialogue and cooperation in illuminating the path toward mutual understanding. By reflecting on the contributions of these historical figures and the ethos of universities as centres of learning, we can pave pathways for future engagements that resonate with the original spirit of inquiry, nurturing a global community that recognises the strength found in shared wisdom.

In closing, this exploration of philosophical exchanges stands as a testament to the potential of collaborative learning. Both faiths have much to gain by examining their historical interactions, for these narratives are more than mere historical records; they are bridges that invite dialogue and unity in the face of contemporary challenges. Appreciating this shared legacy inspires a deep commitment to engaging meaningfully with one another, fostering a future where the past's lessons guide us toward understanding and respect.

Festivals and Traditions

In a world marked by diversity, religious festivals serve as vibrant expressions of faith and community. They are moments when individuals come together to celebrate shared values, cultural heritage, and spiritual beliefs. This subchapter explores the rich tapestry of festivals celebrated in Christianity and Islam, illustrating how holidays such as Christmas, Ramadan, and Eid not only reflect the core principles of each faith but also foster community and interfaith understanding. Through the lens of personal narratives, we will examine how these celebrations create spaces for dialogue, foster deeper connections, and reinforce identity among believers.

The jubilant season of Christmas is a prominent celebration within Christianity, observed annually on December 25th. It marks the nativity of Jesus Christ, recognised by Christians as the Son of God and the Messiah whose teachings form the cornerstone of the faith. Amidst the commercialised hustle and bustle that often accompanies the holiday season, the essence of Christmas is rooted in themes of love, generosity, and forgiveness. It reflects the Christian belief in selfless giving and the importance of compassion, a sentiment articulated beautifully in the Gospel of Luke.

"For unto you is born this day in the city of David a Saviour, which is Christ the Lord" (Luke 2:11). This announcement emphasises the joyous nature of the celebration, inviting Christians to reflect on the profound impact of Jesus' birth on humanity.

Christianity and Islam - Two paths, One Purpose

In many households, the Christmas season commences with the tradition of Advent, a time of preparation that leads up to the holiday. Families light candles on an Advent wreath, symbolising hope and divine light entering the world. The weeks leading up to Christmas are filled with anticipation, as believers engage in various customs, such as decorating their homes with ornaments, singing carols that recount the Nativity story, and participating in religious services.

A personal account from Sarah, a devout Christian, brings the essence of Christmas to life: "Every year, our family gathers on Christmas Eve to share a meal and read the biblical stories of Jesus' birth. It's a time of togetherness, and we always set aside a moment to reflect on the true meaning of Christmas. For us, it's not just about the gifts or the festivities but about honouring the gift of love that Jesus represents."

As Sarah's story illustrates, Christmas serves as a moment for renewal, a time for individuals to reconnect with their faith and community. Many Christians extend this spirit of generosity beyond their tables, engaging in outreach efforts to those in need. Charitable giving, food drives, and providing support to those in need become integral to the observance, reinforcing the values of kindness and compassion central to Jesus' teachings.

In contrast, the Islamic festivities of Ramadan and Eid el-Fitr, though distinct, resonate with similar core values of community and spiritual reflection. Ramadan is the ninth month of the Islamic lunar calendar, during which Muslims observe fasting, prayer, reflection, and community. For Muslims, it is a time to meditate on their spiritual growth and connection to Allah (God). Fasting from dawn until sunset, followers abstain from food, drink, and other physical needs, fostering a greater sense of empathy for those less fortunate.

Christianity and Islam - Two paths, One Purpose

Ahmad, a practising Muslim, shares his experience of Ramadan: "Fasting during Ramadan is a journey of the heart and soul. It's not just about abstaining from food; it's about purifying oneself, being grateful for what we have, and remembering those who are less privileged. Each night of Ramadan, our family gathers for Iftar, the meal to break the fast, and it's a joyous occasion filled with laughter and gratitude."

As Ahmad eloquently expresses, Ramadan is not merely an individual journey but a communal experience. Family and friends come together to break their fasts, and mosques become hubs of community activity, offering nightly prayers and supplications. The nightly Taraweeh prayers allow for extended communal worship, uniting individuals in shared devotion. This spirit of togetherness culminates in the celebration of Eid el-Fitr, known as the "Festival of Breaking the Fast."

Eid el-Fitr is a day of joy and thanksgiving, marking the end of Ramadan. It begins with a special prayer service at the mosque, followed by communal feasting and celebrations. The giving of Zakat al-Fitr, a form of charity meant to purify those who fast and assist the needy, embodies the Islamic principle of generosity. Personal narratives during Eid underscore the sense of community, with many families inviting their neighbours, including friends from other faiths, to partake in the celebration.

Aisha, another practising Muslim, recalls her experiences at Eid: "Eid is such a joyous occasion! We dress in our best clothes and visit friends and family, sharing meals and sweets. One of my favourite traditions is to invite our non-Muslim neighbours. It's a great opportunity to share our culture and faith. The smiles and laughter that fill our homes remind me that we are all part of the same humanity."

Aisha's story reveals how Eid festivities transcend religious boundaries, creating a bridge for understanding and friendship. While Christmas and Eid are rooted in distinct religious narratives, the underlying themes of community, generosity, and the celebration of faith resonate deeply across both traditions.

As we explore further, it becomes evident that the significance of these festivals extends beyond their religious roots, serving as catalysts for interfaith dialogue and understanding. For instance, during the Advent season leading to Christmas, some Christian communities engage in interfaith dialogues, inviting Muslims to share in the celebrations and fostering a spirit of mutual respect and understanding.

Similarly, during Ramadan, many mosques open their doors for Iftar gatherings, inviting people of all backgrounds, including Christians and individuals of other faiths, to join in breaking the fast. This practice highlights the value of sharing traditions and fosters relationships based on empathy and respect.

The integration of these celebrations into interfaith dialogue creates opportunities for education and understanding. Conversations about the significance of fasting in Ramadan or the meaning of Christmas not only enrich participants' knowledge but also dismantle preconceived notions about each faith. Such dialogues help challenge stereotypes that often arise from ignorance, offering a glimpse into the beauty and depth of both traditions.

The transformative power of these festivals fosters an environment where individuals can share their experiences, stories, and practices with one another. Through such interactions, the message of love, compassion, and unity becomes palpable, resonating with the shared narrative of humanity.

Christianity and Islam - Two paths, One Purpose

Furthermore, one cannot overlook the role of art and culture in illustrating the values of both faiths during these festivals. From the intricate designs of Christmas ornaments to the beautiful patterns of Islamic calligraphy used in Eid decorations, these expressions of creativity reflect the joy and significance of these occasions.

In many communities, local artists create pieces that celebrate the interconnectedness of these faiths. Through community events that showcase art reflecting Thanksgiving dinners in Christian homes and the spirit of sharing during Eid, attendees experience firsthand how each belief system cherishes similar core values. Festivals serve as avenues for cultural storytelling, showcasing the shared human experience that transcends cultural boundaries.

The narratives surrounding Christmas and Eid el-Fitr reaffirm the importance of nurturing community connections and forging lasting relationships among diverse faiths. As these celebrations unfold each year, they serve as reminders of the profound similarities that exist between Christianity and Islam. Beyond religious differences, the essence lies in the universal themes of love, compassion, and unity.

Through the shared stories of individuals like Sarah, Ahmad, and Aisha, we recognise that festivals are not merely events on the calendar but milestones in the journey of understanding faith and community. They are threads that weave together a rich tapestry of experiences, reminding us that despite our differences, we are united in the pursuit of compassion, respect, and interconnectedness.

As we move forward, we can envision scaffolding for future interfaith collaborations, cultivated through the shared spirit of these festivals. By gathering to celebrate, learn, and engage with one another, we enhance our collective understanding and reinforce the values that unite us all.

Ultimately, exploring the significance of Christmas, Ramadan, and Eid el-Fitr illuminates the beautiful intersections between Christianity and Islam. As we witness the joy of community celebrations, let us continue to foster dialogue and understanding, nurturing the bonds that connect us in our shared humanity.

Navigating Divergence: Key Beliefs

The Nature of God

The exploration of the concept of God serves as a foundational element in understanding both Christianity and Islam, as it not only defines the core beliefs of each faith but also shapes the lives of millions who follow these teachings. Despite their shared Abrahamic lineage, the two religions present markedly different theological perspectives, particularly concerning the nature and attributes of God. This subchapter aims to explore these distinctions in depth, with a focus on the Christian doctrine of the Trinity and the strict monotheism espoused in Islam. By incorporating insights from both the Practising Muslim and the Devout Christian, we can foster a respectful dialogue that enhances comprehension and encourages interfaith discourse.

To lay the groundwork for this discussion, let us first examine the fundamental beliefs regarding God in Islam. For Muslims, Allah is not only a name but also a representation of the ultimate reality. The meaning of Allah, derived from the Arabic language, signifies the one true God, who is merciful, compassionate, and omnipotent. The Qur'an, which is considered the verbatim word of God as revealed to the Prophet Muhammad, encapsulates this understanding. The opening chapter, **Al-Fatiha**, begins with praises to Allah, reinforcing His uniqueness and oneness.

The Islamic worldview clearly articulates the concept of Tawhid, the absolute oneness of God. Tawhid serves as the cornerstone of

Islamic theology, emphasising that God is singular, without partners or equals. This uncompromising monotheism permeates every aspect of a Muslim's faith and practice. As the Practising Muslim shares, "To believe in Allah is to wholly submit to His will and acknowledge that He has no peers. This belief shapes how I live my life, guiding my actions toward righteousness and justice."

Conversely, in Christianity, the understanding of God is encapsulated in the doctrine of the Trinity, which maintains that God exists as three distinct persons: the Father, the Son, and the Holy Spirit. This complex theological concept is addressed in the New Testament, where various passages provide insights into the relationship between these divine persons. For the Devout Christian, the Trinity is not merely a theological abstraction but a lived experience that shapes their relationship with God. "When I pray, I engage with each person of the Trinity. I speak to the Father, petitioning Him for guidance. I thank the Son for His sacrifice and seek the Spirit's comfort and wisdom in my daily life," he explains.

This conception of God as a triune being distinguishes Christianity from Islam significantly. While Christians assert the co-equality and co-eternity of the three persons of the Trinity, Muslims regard any attempt to assign partners or associates to God as a fundamental misunderstanding of monotheism. The Qur'an explicitly addresses this in several verses, stating that God is unique and indivisible. An example can be found in Surah Al-Ikhlas, where it is said: "Say, 'He is Allah, [who is] One, Allah, the Eternal Refuge. He neither begets nor is born, nor is there to Him any equivalent.'" This concise declaration affirms the Islamic position on monotheism and effectively opposes the Christian framework of the Trinity.

It is vital to recognise that both faiths communicate their understanding of God through distinct lenses shaped by their respective scriptures and traditions. The Bible offers numerous references that have historically been interpreted to support the concept of the Trinity. Passages such as Matthew 28:19, where Jesus instructs his disciples to baptise in the name of the Father, the Son, and the Holy Spirit, are pivotal to the Christian understanding of God's nature. However, the Devout Christian candidly acknowledges the challenges associated with articulating the doctrine of the Trinity, stating, "It is a mystery that cannot be fully comprehended by human understanding. Yet, through faith, we see the relationship between the three persons as foundational to our salvation and understanding of divine love."

In stark contrast, Islamic theology places an unwavering focus on the oneness of God. The Practising Muslim, reflecting on this belief, mentions, "In my daily prayers, I emphasise the singularity of Allah, reminding myself that He alone is worthy of worship, and I strive to steer clear of any notion that could dilute this belief. It brings me comfort to know that my faith is rooted in a clear and uncompromised monotheism."

Discussing the attributes of God reveals further distinctions and similarities between the two faiths. Both Christianity and Islam affirm key characteristics of God, such as omniscience, omnipotence, and benevolence. However, the expressions of these attributes may reflect differing cultural and theological contexts. For instance, in Christianity, God's love is often associated with the sacrificial actions of Jesus Christ, who is viewed as God's ultimate expression of love toward humanity. The Devout Christian articulates this concept succinctly: "Through the life, death, and resurrection of Jesus, I see God's love personified. It's about relationships and grace. I am invited into a deep communion with Him through Christ."

In Islam, God's mercy is similarly emphasised, often highlighted in the opening declaration of the Qur'an—"In the name of Allah, the Most Gracious, the Most Merciful." The Practising Muslim notes, "Allah's mercy is vast, encompassing all creation, and it is a reminder that we, too, must embody mercy in our actions. The understanding of God's attributes guides us towards living lives infused with compassion and justice."

Both religions also acknowledge God's immanence and transcendence, though they articulate these experiences differently. In Christianity, the belief in Jesus as the incarnate God brings a profound, immediate and personal connection to the divine. For the Devout Christian, this idea is the essence of faith: "God is not distant; He became one of us. This incarnational theology informs how I see the world and interact with others."

Islam, while recognising Allah's closeness to His creation through the concept of Him being closer than one's jugular vein (Qur'an 50:16), maintains a distinction that emphasises God's otherness and transcendence as a safeguard against any diminishment of His divine nature. The Practising Muslim states, "While Allah is near, He is also beyond our complete understanding. This balance is crucial in how I view my relationship with Him—one of submission, respect, and love."

The discussion on God's nature inevitably leads to the examination of salvation and how both faiths perceive humanity's relationship with the divine. In Christianity, salvation is primarily through grace — a gift received through faith in Jesus Christ. The Devout Christian shares, "It is not by works alone, but through the grace of God that I am saved. This understanding shapes my worldview; it drives me to share that grace with others."

Christianity and Islam - Two paths, One Purpose

In contrast, Islam introduces the concept of balance between God's mercy and justice. Actions and intentions hold significant weight in the Islamic faith, exemplifying how believers navigate their relationship with Allah through both worship and adherence to moral principles. The Practising Muslim explains, "We are judged not only on our beliefs but on how those beliefs translate into action. Islam calls for accountability, and this relationship compels me to strive for righteousness."

As these distinct perspectives on God's nature unfold through dialogue, it enhances an understanding rooted in respect and compassion. Both the Practising Muslim and the Devout Christian acknowledge that their beliefs lead them to seek justice, mercy, and the betterment of humanity. "It is the love for God that drives genuinely faithful people to act justly and offer compassion to others, regardless of their faith," asserts the Devout Christian.

"It is our shared commitment to a higher moral calling that allows us to bridge the gaps where theological differences exist," adds the Practising Muslim, highlighting the possibility of collaboration between faiths based on shared values.

The conversation surrounding God's nature also incites reflections on contemporary issues facing both religions. Sectarian divides within Christianity and Islam can complicate the understanding of God, leading to divergent interpretations and practices. The Devout Christian argues, "It's essential for Christians to remember that our interpretations should reflect Christ's love and humility, seeking unity within our diversity." The Practising Muslim reciprocates, stating, "As Muslims, we must acknowledge the importance of unity while also respecting various interpretations that arise through cultural and historical contexts of our faith."

Christianity and Islam - Two paths, One Purpose

This call for unity, despite divergent beliefs regarding God's nature, underscores the imperative of interfaith dialogue. By recognising the core principles — love, mercy, and justice — that both faiths elevate, we can foster collaborative efforts aimed at addressing global challenges. The Practising Muslim reflects, "Engaging in dialogue about God helps us to empathise with each other's journey and ultimately work together towards the common good." The Devout Christian concurs, noting, "It is in the exploration of our differences and commonalities that we find pathways to peace and understanding. Collaborating as people of faith will enable us to witness the love of God in action."

The essence of this dialogue, enriched by the contributions of both individuals, allows us to appreciate the nuanced and multifaceted perspectives on God within Christianity and Islam. It illustrates that while distinct theological frameworks exist, they are not insurmountable barriers. Instead, they can serve as starting points for a richer discourse that honours each faith's uniqueness while discovering bridges of empathy and shared values.

Ultimately, the journey of understanding the nature of God in Christianity and Islam may not yield definitive answers, but it serves as an invaluable pathway to fostering respect and compassion. Both the Practising Muslim and the Devout Christian exemplify how engaging with these complex theological dimensions can open doors to deeper connections, propelling individuals of diverse faiths toward a more united and compassionate existence. This exploration reinforces a vital understanding: while our conceptualisations of God may differ, the qualities of justice, mercy, and compassion are universal, inviting all of humanity to participate in a dialogue rich with possibility for mutual respect and understanding.

Salvation and the Afterlife

In the landscape of faith, few concepts are as pivotal and complex as those surrounding salvation and the afterlife. Christianity and Islam, two of the world's major religions, present distinct yet interwoven beliefs regarding these profound topics. Both faiths grapple with questions of sin, redemption, and the eternal journey that awaits human souls after death. This exploration aims to reveal how these beliefs not only inform the doctrines of each religion but also influence the moral compasses and daily lives of their adherents.

Central to both Christianity and Islam is the understanding of sin. In Christianity, sin is seen as a separation from God, an obstacle that disrupts the relationship between humanity and the divine. The origin of sin is often traced back to the Fall of Man, as told in the Genesis narrative, where Adam and Eve's disobedience led to the introduction of sin into the world. This concept of original sin is foundational in Christian thought, leading to the belief that all human beings are born with a sinful nature. Therefore, the need for salvation becomes paramount; it is not merely an option, but a necessity for reconciling with God.

In contrast, Islam teaches that humans are born free of sin. The Islamic concept of sin is not inherited but committed through conscious choices. Each person is accountable for their actions, and while sin may lead one away from Allah, it is within everyone's capacity to seek forgiveness. In Islam, the emphasis is on personal responsibility and the merciful nature of Allah, who awaits repentance from His followers. This distinction reflects a different approach to the relationship between humanity and the divine: for Christians, a saviour is needed to bridge the gap created by sin, while in Islam, Allah's mercy and the individual's efforts are the keys to salvation.

The role of Jesus in Christian theology further complicates the discussion of salvation. For Christians, Jesus is viewed as the incarnate Son of God, whose sacrificial death and subsequent resurrection provide the pathway to salvation. This belief is encapsulated in the doctrine of atonement, which posits that through Jesus' sacrifice, believers are offered forgiveness for their sins and the promise of eternal life. The New Testament is filled with passages that underscore this belief, including John 3:16, which states, "For God so loved the world that he gave his one and only Son, that whoever believes in him shall not perish but have eternal life."

Conversely, in Islam, Jesus (known as Isa) is revered as one of the greatest prophets but is not divine. The Qur'an teaches that Jesus was born of the Virgin Mary and performed miracles, yet he is not the Son of God, and his death is viewed differently. Muslims believe that Jesus was not crucified; instead, he was raised to heaven by Allah, and that he will return on the Day of Judgment as a sign of the end times. In Islamic theology, salvation is achieved through submission to the will of Allah, as articulated in the Five Pillars of Islam, which include faith, prayer, almsgiving, fasting, and pilgrimage.

When considering the afterlife, both faiths present vivid imagery of what is to come after death. Christianity offers a dichotomy between heaven and hell. For Christians, those who accept Christ and live according to His teachings are promised eternal life in heaven, often depicted as a place of joy, peace, and communion with God. Conversely, those who reject Christ or live contrary to his commandments face eternal separation from God in hell, described in various biblical passages as a place of torment and anguish.

Islam, similarly, describes the afterlife in terms of paradise (Jannah) and hell (Jahannam). Jannah is portrayed as a lush garden of pleasures for the faithful who submit to Allah's guidance, fulfil their earthly duties, and live righteously. Jahannam, on the other hand, is a place of punishment for those who deny God, transgress His commands, or lead others astray. The Qur'an describes the afterlife extensively, and Muslims often recite verses that remind them of the temporality of this life and the significance of preparing for the journey after death.

As the afterlife is central to both religions, it informs how adherents navigate their daily lives and make moral choices. For many Christians, the belief in eternal life propels acts of charity, integrity, and a sense of purpose. The desire to be good stewards of the earth and to show kindness to others is rooted in the view that such acts reflect one's faith and relationship with God, ultimately influencing one's standing in the afterlife. The teachings of Jesus, particularly the command to love one's neighbour, serve as guiding principles that shape day-to-day decision-making and interpersonal relationships among believers.

For Muslims, the notion of accountability in the afterlife encourages a life of adherence to Islamic principles and ethical behaviour. The concept of 'ilm (knowledge) catalyses moral living, leading believers to seek righteousness in all aspects of their lives. Each action is weighed on a scale, with the intent (niyyah) behind each deed being crucial. Acts of worship, honesty in trade, familial responsibilities, and social justice play significant roles in determining one's fate in the afterlife. The practice of Zakat, or almsgiving, underscores the communal aspect of faith and the understanding that helping those in need is not only an act of worship but a means of securing favour with Allah.

To illustrate how beliefs in salvation and the afterlife manifest in daily life, the stories of individuals from both faiths offer valuable perspectives. For instance, Sarah, a devout Christian mother, shares her journey of faith. Raised in a church-going household, she recalls attending Sunday services where discussions about heaven and hell were frequently held. She embraces her faith as a guide for her moral decisions, instilling in her children the values of love and compassion. Sarah often reflects **on Matthew 25:40** when volunteering at local shelters, believing that serving the marginalised mirrors her faith's tenets. Her conviction that acts of kindness contribute to her eternal reward fuels her commitment to community service, showing how her understanding of salvation shapes her values and actions.

On the other hand, Ahmed, a practising Muslim, recounts his path to faith and the principles that guide his life choices. Coming from a family that emphasised the importance of education and moral conduct, he understands the significance of salah (prayer) in grounding his spirituality. For Ahmed, maintaining a daily prayer routine is not merely a ritual; it is a conscious engagement with Allah that serves as a reminder of his purpose. His commitment to helping others through charity, particularly Zakat, emerges from his belief that such acts will lead him to Jannah. Ahmed narrates how his involvement in local community outreach programs reflects his dedication to living out Islamic values, emphasising that the concept of accountability shapes his approach to both personal and communal responsibilities.

As we navigate through the theological frameworks of salvation and the afterlife, the importance of life choices becomes clear. Both faiths agree that the decisions made in this life have everlasting consequences, yet the paths to what followers hope to attain differ significantly. The Christian perspective often revolves around the idea of faith in Jesus Christ as the ultimate way, whereas in Islam, righteous living and submission to Allah's will are paramount.

Despite their differences, both sets of beliefs encourage followers to reflect on how they live their lives. The moral imperatives presented in both religions call on adherents to cultivate virtues such as compassion, honesty, and justice. These shared values can serve as a bridge between the two faiths, fostering an understanding that transcends theological divides.

In conclusion, the concepts of salvation and the afterlife within Christianity and Islam are profound and multifaceted, shaped by scriptural teachings, historical contexts, and personal convictions. The exploration of sin, redemption, and the hope for eternal life illustrates how both faiths intertwine in shared human experiences, creating a rich tapestry that reflects the diverse yet similar ways people seek meaning and connection to the divine. Examination of personal stories further reveals the profound impact that beliefs about salvation have on everyday lives, shaping moral choices and community interactions. By acknowledging these distinctions and similarities, followers of both faiths can find opportunities for dialogue, understanding, and unity, paving the way for a future where shared values guide actions in a world often marked by division.

Role of Scriptures in Daily Life

In the intersecting narratives of Christianity and Islam, scripture is not merely a collection of ancient texts; it is the living word that shapes the lives of believers. Both the Bible and the Qur'an serve as essential cornerstones of faith, informing the daily experiences, moral decisions, and community connections of countless individuals worldwide. This subchapter will explore how these sacred texts manifest in everyday life, illuminating their practical applications while sharing personal accounts that reflect their transformative power.

For Christians, the Bible stands as a testament to faith—a wide-ranging anthology encompassing history, poetry, prophecy, and teachings. Its influence is permeable; it touches moments of joy, grief, hope, and despair. In the words of James, a devout follower from a small Midwestern town, "The Bible is my compass. It directs my path and illuminates the darkness. On days when I feel lost, I turn to its pages and find my way again."

James vividly recalls a period when he battled uncertainty in his career. He felt stagnant and uninspired, searching for direction. It was at this juncture that he revisited Proverbs, where he found wisdom rekindled through verses that reminded him to trust in the Lord's plan. Inspired, he embarked on new endeavours, taking calculated risks and eventually finding fulfilment in a path he had not previously considered.

In another personal testimony, Fatima, a practising Muslim from Egypt, articulates her experiences with the Qur'an in her daily practice. "When I read the Qur'an, it's not just words on a page. It's guidance for how to live, how to treat others, and how to remain steadfast in faith, especially in challenging moments," she comments. Fatima recounts a time when her family faced societal pressures due to their beliefs. In the face of adversity, reciting verses from Surah Al-Baqarah fortified her resolve and fostered a spirit of compassion among her family members.

Christianity and Islam - Two paths, One Purpose

The transformative power of scriptures suggests that they act not solely as spiritual sustenance but also as a nurturing presence that fosters communal relationships. In both faiths, holy scriptures inspire approaches to charity and service that reinforce the values of empathy, compassion, and community cohesion.

In Christianity, Jesus's teachings encapsulate an ethos of love and kindness, which transcends mere worship to influence believers' interactions with others. The Sermon on the Mount, recorded in the Gospel of Matthew, resonates as a guiding narrative for countless Christians, inspiring them to embody values of mercy, humility, and ethical living. For Ann, a youth pastor in a diverse urban community, mentoring young adults often revolves around the principles found in these teachings. She observes, "When we engage with scripture together, we not only learn about our faith; we also learn how to treat each other with respect and kindness, regardless of our differences. The Bible's messages resonate in every volunteer project we undertake."

Meanwhile, the Qur'an similarly emphasises the significance of charity and social justice, as enshrined in its teachings. The practice of Zakat (charitable giving) is a fundamental pillar of Islam, deeply woven into the fabric of a Muslim's daily life. Khalid, a community organiser in a bustling metropolis, recounts how he and his local congregation come together each month to distribute Zakat to those in need. "The Qur'an reminds us constantly of our responsibility to help others, to uplift the downtrodden. These gatherings empower us to act on our faith, turning scripture into tangible action," he explains. Khalid's sentiment exemplifies how the Qur'an directs believers to build a compassionate society, echoing common values of both faiths.

Christianity and Islam - Two paths, One Purpose

As we explore the practical applications of scripture, it is essential to acknowledge the role of community in nurturing these values. Both the Bible and the Qur'an emphasise the importance of gatherings, whether for worship, study, or fellowship. These communal interactions create avenues for believers to share insights, discuss scriptures, and support one another in their spiritual journeys.

Let us turn to Rita, who participates in a bi-weekly Bible study with a group of friends. "In our meetings, the Bible is always our focal point. We dive deep into scripture, share our struggles, and uplift each other, practising what we learn from the Word. I don't just read, I live what I learn through our fellowship," she shares with enthusiasm. The closeness forged within this group reflects that scripture shapes the very fabric of their communal lives, guiding them in moments of both difficulty and joy.

Similarly, Muhammad describes how his mosque facilitates community gatherings centred around the Qur'an. "Understanding the Qur'an in tandem with others deepens my knowledge and strengthens my faith. We learn the significance of verses and how they apply to our lives, with everyone contributing their perspective," he notes. This group dynamic fosters a sense of belonging that solidifies the roles of each believer as part of a larger spiritual family.

In regard to daily routines, the rituals surrounding scripture reading or recitation serve as focal points, often marking transitions and moments of reflection. For Muslims, the practice of praying five times a day involves reciting portions of the Qur'an, weaving spirituality seamlessly into the everyday activities of life. Zainab, a dedicated mother, shares how these practices shape not only her life but also her children's. "In our household, leading prayers and reciting the Qur'an together cultivates a sense of peace and purpose. It teaches my kids gratitude and patience—values that guide their actions outside our walls, too," she says.

Similarly, Christians often integrate scripture into their daily lives through prayer and meditation, acknowledging its role as a touchstone amidst chaos. Daniel, who works as a nurse, remarks, "Before each shift, I take a moment to read a chapter from the Bible. It calms my spirits and reminds me of my purpose in caring for others. It's more than practice—it's essential for my mental and emotional health." Daniel's example showcases how scriptural insights provide guidance, grounding believers in their workplace and elevating their service toward others.

Moreover, the presence of scripture in life events—from marriages to funerals—reflects its profound authority and meaning. In Christianity, many couples incorporate Bible passages into their wedding ceremonies, selecting verses that speak to love, commitment, and unity. The chosen scriptures become vows enshrined in a sacred context, elevating their bond with divine blessings. This act signifies the integration of divine teachings into the most personal aspects of life.

On the Islamic side, reciting specific verses during weddings and memorial services also embodies the significance of community ties, familial bonds, and submission to God's will. Notably, during a family wedding ceremony, Fatih recalls the invocation of Surah Al-Fatihah as a central element, stating, "We invite blessings upon the marriage through the Qur'an. It strengthens our family ties, reminding us of the importance of faith in every aspect of life."

As these personal accounts reveal, scriptures extend their influence beyond individual practice. They forge connections across generations, enriching the collective wisdom and experiences shared within families and communities. Grandparents pass on teachings from scriptures to their grandchildren, fostering a continuity of faith that brings warmth, guidance, and memories bound together by the sacred texts.

When reflecting on how scriptures mould ethical values in everyday interactions, both the Bible and the Qur'an serve as moral compasses, guiding adherents toward righteous behaviour. Whether through parables, commandments, or divine guidance, followers draw upon these texts to navigate life's complexities.

Maria, a schoolteacher, epitomises this integration of scripture into moral decision-making. "When teaching my students values, I often reference the Good Samaritan story to inspire kindness toward others, irrespective of their background or beliefs. The moral lessons from the Bible become a backdrop for fostering empathy and respect in the classroom," she explains. Maria's experiences reflect how scripture shapes everyday conduct, emphasising the inherent connection to ethical frameworks.

Conversely, Inara illustrates similar perspectives rooted in the Qur'an, as she shares her approach to educating youth. "I teach my students to follow the principles of justice and equity, as emphasised in various verses. Stories from the Qur'an inspire them to be honest, kind, and to stand up for what's right, promoting values that lead to healthier communities."

The symbiotic relationship between scripture and ethical guidance is reciprocal; values embedded in these texts become evident as constituents engage respectfully within their societies. This leads to a unified message that encourages goodwill, social responsibility, and peace between different faiths.

Christianity and Islam - Two paths, One Purpose

The role of scriptures extends beyond simply providing guidance; they also underscore the necessity of faith in the daily fabric of life. Personal afflictions, societal challenges, and individual adversities are met with scriptural solace, leading individuals to turn their struggles into testimony. For Claire, who faced a personal crisis, turning to the Bible offered profound consolation. "In the depths of my grief, Psalm 23 brought comfort and a reminder that I am never alone in my sorrow," she confided. This scriptural promise resonated deeply with her, providing strength and a sense of divine companionship amid despair.

In a similar vein, Rami candidly reflects on navigating personal challenges through the Qur'an. "When I lost my job last year, facing uncertainty was daunting. Reading verses on patience and trust in Allah supported my resilience, giving me hope when I felt lost. Those words transformed my perspective, directing me toward new possibilities," Rami shares.

Such reflections embody the affirming power of holy scriptures, depicting them as sanctuaries in turbulent times, reminding believers of the enduring aspects of faith and community support.

Lastly, the engagement with sacred texts serves as a prophetic reminder of the call to justice, righteousness, and unity. In an increasingly divisive world, individuals from both faiths find that scripture enshrines the values necessary to navigate societal landscapes fraught with conflict. Initiatives emerging from both Christian and Muslim communities that address social justice illustrate how interpretations of scripture empower collaborative endeavours for a common cause.

For example, various interfaith organisations focus on pressing societal issues like poverty and discrimination, citing scriptures to guide their mission. During a community forum, members of diverse faith backgrounds gathered to discuss progressive actions inspired by their respective teachings. In this space, interfaith dialogue flourished, with representatives from both sides invoking scriptural precedents for peace and cooperation. These interactions underscore the relevancy of scripture as not merely historical artefacts but as living guides informing contemporary social justice movements.

The role of scriptures in daily life echoes the underlying imperative to build bridges of compassion and understanding. Both the Bible and the Qur'an provide powerful modalities for navigating personal, communal, and societal realms while inspiring believers to forge connections that transcend religious boundaries. As they revolve around shared teachings of love, justice, and service, each faith offers inclusivity, inviting adherents to witness their scriptures alive in their everyday experiences.

For in doing so, Christians and Muslims alike find their paths intertwined, acknowledging that while their texts differ in doctrine and interpretation, the transformative power of scripture remains constant, guiding faith-forward amid diversity.

In conclusion, the invaluable testimonies and narratives shared in this subchapter demonstrate the profound impact of scriptures on shaping lives. The Bible and the Qur'an embody teachings woven into the very fabric of daily existence, serving believers in their decisions, interactions, and collective initiatives. In illuminating the personal and communal applications of these sacred texts, we find that they are not merely pages filled with writing; they are double-edged swords of hope, guidance, and unifying compassion. As the threads of faith continue to entwine, may they serve as bridges fostering dialogue and connection across the vast tapestry of humanity.

The Mystical Winds of Faith and Practice

Rituals of Worship

In the vast tapestry of human spirituality, rituals of worship serve as the threads that bind individuals to their faith and one another. In examining the rituals practised in Christianity and Islam, we uncover a profound exploration of identity, community, and devotion. Rituals, as expressions of innate human longing for connection with the divine, reveal both the shared threads and distinct patterns of these two great religions. Through prayer, community gatherings, and the rites of passage, followers of both faiths engage with the transcendental, creating a sense of belonging that echoes through generations.

Rituals in both Christianity and Islam form the backbone of religious practice, providing structured outlets for worship, connection, and reflection. From the rhythmic cadence of prayers to the communal celebrations of holy days, worship brings faith to life in tangible ways. In this subchapter, we will delve into significant rituals, exploring their roots, their communal significance, and the personal narratives that illustrate their impact on believers' lives.

Salah: The Islamic Prayer

At the heart of Islamic worship lies Salah, the ritual prayer performed five times a day. Considered one of the Five Pillars of Islam, Salah is not merely a routine; it is a profound act of devotion that reorients the believer's focus toward Allah, the all-powerful

God. Each of the five prayers—Fajr, Dhuhr, Asr, Maghrib, and Isha—corresponds to specific times throughout the day, marking the transitions of daily life with sacred pauses.

Morning prayer at dawn, Fajr, begins the day with an intimate connection to the divine, as believers gather in solitude or within the congregation for the opening verses of the Qur'an. It is often described as a gentle awakening, both physically and spiritually. The quietness of the early morning enhances the experience, allowing practitioners to reflect on gratitude and purpose as they prepare to face the day ahead.

In contrast, Dhuhr occurs at noon, serving as a reminder to reflect amid the busyness of life. As the sun reaches its zenith, Muslims pause to realign their intentions. The act of prayer becomes a collective experience as the community gathers, shoulder to shoulder, in the mosque or at home. This moment of unity underscores the significance of community in Islam, where worship is not merely a personal affair but a collective expression of faith.

As believers bow and prostrate, the movements of Salah—standing, bowing, prostrating, and sitting—symbolically illustrate humility before Allah. This physical expression merges the metaphysical with the tangible, linking the believer's body to spiritual intent. An inspiring narrative from Fatimah, a practising Muslim, illustrates this beautifully:

"When I stand in prayer, I feel connected to my roots. It's as if I am following in the footsteps of my ancestors who prayed in the same way, facing the same Qibla. Each bow and prostration reminds me of my purpose and the community to which I belong. In the mosque with my fellow believers, I truly feel the power of unity, and it reinforces my identity as a Muslim woman."

The Asr prayer in the late afternoon becomes a personal pause, an acknowledgement of the hustle and bustle of everyday life while reinforcing prioritisation toward faith. As the shadows lengthen, believers acknowledge their need for spiritual sustenance before they approach the close of the day. Maghrib, the sunset prayer, ushers in an end-of-day reflection, the transition from the light of day into the quieting embrace of night. Evening prayers may serve a dual purpose: a way to express gratitude for the day's blessings and a moment to seek forgiveness for missteps.

Isha, the final prayer of the day, carries a unique sense of closure, closing the chapter of daily life. The stillness that surrounds evening prayers deepens the reflective spirit, allowing participants to contemplate not only their relationship with Allah but also the ties that bind them to their community.

The Mass: A Christian Sacrament

In Christianity, the Mass or Eucharist stands at the centre of communal worship. This sacred ritual represents the culmination of faith in action, as believers partake in the body and blood of Christ, commemorating the Last Supper. Catholics regard the Mass as a sacrament that mandates both personal conversion and communal shared faith, encouraging attendees to nourish their spiritual well-being. From the opening hymn to the final blessing, every aspect of the Mass serves a distinct purpose, drawing the congregation into a sacred narrative.

The structure of the Mass unfolds in two primary parts: the Liturgy of the Word and the Liturgy of the Eucharist. The first part emphasises Scripture, whereby readings from the Bible resonate with the believers, reinforcing not only their knowledge but also their faith. The congregational responses and hymns emphasise the communal experience. Here, the faithful find strength in collective worship, echoing shared struggles and hopes:

"Just like the prayers in our hearts, the readings in the Liturgy provide me with a deeper understanding of God's love for me. Even when I come to Mass with personal challenges, hearing the Word shared by my brothers and sisters reminds me that faith is not a solitary path but a journey we share," shares Michael, a devout Christian.

The Eucharistic celebration entails the culmination of liturgical action, as the bread and wine, believed to become the body and blood of Christ, highlight the profound mystery of faith. The act of communion extends beyond individual reception; it reinforces the unity of the Body of Christ, a metaphor for the Church itself. The sharing of the Eucharist directly relates to the intrinsic idea of community, where the faithful gather to partake in a sacramental meal, thereby fostering connections among themselves.

Communal Aspects and Self-Identity

Both Salah and Mass are not merely acts of individual devotion; they intrinsically embody the essence of community within each faith. As services unfold, they illustrate not only respect for tradition but also the growth of community and identity.

In Islam, collective prayers amplify the experience of worship, particularly during Jummah (Friday prayer). As practitioners come together, echoing a shared sense of purpose, the communal aspects of Salah flourish. Ustad Omar, an Imam, emphasises, "During Jummah, it's a reminder that we are all part of something greater than ourselves. It's not simply a gathering; it's a reaffirmation of our faith, a ceremony that binds us."

Christianity and Islam - Two paths, One Purpose

In Christianity, the Mass acts as a unifying force that extends beyond Sunday worship. Churches often serve as community centres—spaces where believers gather for social programs, mutual support, and shared initiatives. For church members, this broader context underscores the significance of understanding oneself within a community of faith. Sister Mary, a community leader in her church, underscores this sentiment:

"When I serve in my church, I don't just feel like a part of a group; I experience a sense of belonging and purpose. The Mass is just the beginning, as it inspires me to connect with others throughout the week, helping those in need and supporting our community's growth."

The linkage of individual self-identity to religious rituals emphasises the age-old themes of belonging. As individuals engage with their faith, a cycle of personal and communal growth emerges, where the experiences and practices reinforce the spirit of identity within the frames of both Christianity and Islam.

Rituals During Holy Days

Both faiths celebrate holy days that serve as focal points for communal worship. In Islam, Ramadan stands out as a period of fasting, reflection, and prayer each year. The Islamic practice of fasting, particularly during the month of Ramadan, transforms daily routines into sacred engagements. The communal iftar—the meal breaking the fast at sunset—amplifies feelings of solidarity among Muslims.

As dusk falls and families and friends gather, the breaking of the fast symbolises unity and gratitude. Personal narratives blend with the communal fabric at iftar gatherings, as Fatima reflects:

"During Ramadan, our iftars become more than just meals; they turn into opportunities for sharing love and connection. Each bite feels special as we gather around the table, breaking bread and sharing stories. It's about more than what we eat; it's about who we are together."

Christianity reflects this communal aspect through celebrations such as Christmas and Easter. At Christmas, the gathering of families in churches brings warmth and joy, creating opportunities for community engagement through light, music, and storytelling. The Christmas Mass invites congregants to celebrate the birth of Jesus while reflecting on the significance of hope and renewal.

During Easter, the Paschal vigil becomes a transformative evening for Christians across denominations. The liturgical celebrations invite believers to partake in the joy of resurrection, often beginning in darkness and culminating in the light of the risen Christ. In hometown settings, Easter sunrise services exemplify the beauty of worshipping together at dawn, encapsulating both hope and new beginnings:

"As we stand together on a chilly Easter morning, the sunrise feels like more than just a new day; it embodies the promise of life and resurrection. Singing hymns together, I feel uplifted by our collective belief and love for Christ," says Mary, a witness to the poignant moment.

Rituals of Life Cycle Events

Both Christianity and Islam emphasise life-cycle events, marking significant milestones through communal rituals that connect individuals to their faith and community. In Islam, the Aqiqah ceremony held after the birth of a child illustrates the joy of new life, complemented by an act of sacrifice shared with the community. Families come together to celebrate the newborn's arrival, ushering the child into the ummah (community) while underscoring the implications of faith.

"When my son was born, the Aqiqah wasn't just about the sheep we sacrificed; it symbolised our gratitude and responsibility. Friends and family gathered to sing blessings onto him, wrapping him in love and connection to our faith since the very start of his life," relays Zara, a Muslim mother reflecting on her son's celebration.

In Christianity, baptism marks a definitive commitment to the faith for both infants and adults. This sacred ritual symbolises cleansing and renewal, often held in community gatherings where families and friends are invited. For many, baptism represents an initiation into a communal life of faith, where the congregation pledges to support one another in their spiritual journeys.

"When my daughter was baptised, I felt a surge of community warmth around us. It wasn't just a ritual for her; it was the community welcoming her into a journey of faith, where we'd help guide her. Seeing everyone gather felt like being enveloped in a shared hug of faith," shares Kristina, a mother whose heart swells with pride as she reflects on the day.

Rituals of Healing and Remembrance

The roles of rituals in healing and remembrance within both faiths also illuminate the significance these practices hold in participants' lives. In Islam, visiting the sick and attending funerals are rituals underscored by community remembrance. Providing your presence to someone ill is seen as an act of compassion, enriched by prayers offered for their recovery.

The ritual of Janazah (funeral prayer) stands as a poignant reminder of life's transience while also emphasising the community's role in supporting families in mourning. The prayers offered during Janazah serve not only as solace for the grieving but also as a communal reaffirmation of the faith that binds believers together.

"When I lost my father, the support from my community felt monumental. Each prayer offered during the Janazah was a healing balm, carrying my family along in moments of sorrow. I remember every hug and kind word. In these moments, I truly felt the embrace of our shared faith," reflects Ahmed, recalling the comfort found in communal rituals.

In Christianity (Catholic), rites of passage, memorials, and funeral services provide avenues for both individual and collective mourning. The ritual of remembrance, particularly on All Souls' Day or the feast of All Saints, invites communities to come together in honouring those who have passed. Candles are lit, prayers lifted, and memories shared, reinforcing connections among the living and the departed.

"On All Souls' Day, I am reminded how intertwined our journeys are, even with those who have gone before us. Lighting candles for my loved ones connects me with their memory, and standing together with others battling similar grief offers a sense of peace," shares Clara, a devoted church member.

Conclusion

The rituals of worship, prayer, and remembrance within Christianity and Islam weave together profound expressions of faith and community. They serve as vital conduits for believers to articulate their commitment, whether through the salawat in Salah, the sanctity of the Mass, or communal gatherings during holy days.

Through shared practices, personal narratives highlight how rituals profoundly shape identity, forging connections not only with the divine but also among community members. As we reflect on these sacred traditions, we witness how faith transcends divisions, emphasising collective journeys toward an understanding of love, hope, and unity—a reminder that within the intricacies of worship, both Christianity and Islam stand united in their quest for divine connection and community.

The deep-rooted rituals, whether embedded in daily practice or punctuated by special occasions, reveal the essence of what it means to belong, forming a communion of faith that echoes through time and resonates with the shared human experience.

The Role of Spirituality

Spirituality often transcends the doctrinal boundaries set by structured religion, offering a more personal exploration of faith and a deeper connection to the divine. In the intertwined tapestry of Christianity and Islam, spirituality manifests in various forms, each distinct yet remarkably similar, beckoning adherents towards love, peace, and understanding. This subchapter will explore the spiritual dimensions of both faiths, illustrating how they guide believers in their journeys towards inner peace, love for God, and higher consciousness.

Sufism, often referred to as Islamic mysticism, emphasises a personal, direct experience of God. This tradition encourages believers to seek a deeper relationship through practices such as dhikr (remembrance), poetry, music, and dance. The mystics, or

Sufis, believe that through the purification of the heart and the surrender of the self, one can attain a state of divine love and unity with God. A famous Sufi poet, Rumi, encapsulated this idea beautifully in his verses, emphasising that love is the fundamental force that binds the soul to the divine.

"The wound is the place where the Light enters you," Rumi wrote, reflecting the notion that our struggles and pains are essential in guiding us toward divine understanding. Through this lens, suffering is not merely a burden but a catalyst for personal transformation and spiritual growth.

In personal testimonies shared within the Sufi community, individuals recount their experiences of divine encounters that transformed their lives. Fatima, a Sufi practitioner from Morocco, shared her journey of discovery as she navigated her faith amidst personal turmoil. "In the depths of my sorrow, I found solace in the songs of the mystics—each note resonated with a part of my soul I had long neglected. It was as if I were transported to a realm where love and light lit the darkest corners of my heart, showing me the way back to God."

Such narratives illustrate the pivotal role of music and art in Sufi spirituality, serving not only as expressions of devotion but also as avenues for profound internal dialogue. The Sufi tradition teaches that engaging in these spiritual arts can elevate the soul and foster a sense of communion with the divine.

Across the spectrum of Christian faith, Mystical Theology similarly seeks to explore and deepen the relationship between the believer and God. This tradition is characterised by contemplative practices aimed at attaining a direct experience of God's presence. Mystical theologians such as Saint John of the Cross and Teresa of Ávila laid the foundation for a path that leads from inner stillness to divine revelations.

Saint John of the Cross, renowned for his writings on the Dark Night of the Soul, spoke to the profound journey of spiritual purification required to approach God. He described the soul's journey as a transformative process, where the illumination of divine truth emerges only after one has traversed the shadows of one's inner struggles. The trials of the spirit serve as purifying fires, stripping away distractions and leading the soul closer to its Creator.

In recounting her spiritual journey, Maria, a practitioner of Christian mysticism, shared, "My encounters with the divine were not always easy; there were moments of darkness that felt unending. But in that darkness, I learned to listen. I found a still, small voice guiding me. It was wrapped in comfort, resilience, and an ineffable sense of love."

This quest for intimacy with God fosters a sense of belonging and community amongst practitioners of Mystical Theology. Shared practices such as meditation, contemplative prayer, and silent reflection connect the individual not only to God but also to others who bear similar spiritual burdens.

While Sufism and Mystical Theology may seem divergent in their practices and representations, both emphasise the importance of love as the foundation of their spiritual journeys. Love in both traditions transcends mere adherence to rules or rituals; it is a transformative force that propels believers closer to understanding the divine.

The Harmoniser, with a keen sense of the spiritual landscape, observes that spirituality in both faiths urges followers to cultivate a heartfelt connection with God, nurturing the belief that divine love is synonymous with eternal peace. This understanding resonates deeply within the hearts of practitioners, guiding them in their pursuit of spiritual authenticity.

The Harmoniser reflects on the shared essence of humility in both mystic traditions. In Sufism, the path towards divine love is often paved with the acknowledgement of one's insignificance in the grand scheme of existence. Sufi masters teach that the ego, or nafs, must be tamed to perceive the presence of the divine. As a Sufi saying suggests, "You must be empty to be filled." This emptiness is not about loss; instead, it prepares the heart to receive God's infinite love and grace.

Similarly, in Christian Mystical Theology, humility is paramount. The understanding that every individual, regardless of their past, can approach God with an open heart fosters an ethos of inclusivity. It guarantees that no one is inherently forsaken but simply on a unique journey toward understanding God's infinite compassion.

The Harmoniser recalls a meeting where practitioners from both faiths shared their spiritual experiences. Each story illuminated shared human truths, emphasising compassion, forgiveness, and the collective quest for peace. These interfaith conversations revealed to participants an unexpectedly similar core: both traditions celebrate the journey of spiritual awakening and the effect of grace upon the believer's life.

As individuals develop their spiritual practices within these frameworks, they often encounter the concept of inner peace—a key aspiration shared by both Christians and Muslims. The Harmoniser emphasises that attaining inner peace is not a one-time event; rather, it is an ongoing journey that requires dedication, self-reflection, patience, and profound love.

Christianity and Islam - Two paths, One Purpose

One of the most beautiful dimensions of spirituality among practitioners is the emphasis on service as an extension of inner peace. Misha, an Islamic humanitarian worker, shares her insights into how her spiritual practices have guided her in serving others. "Every prayer I offer, every moment of remembrance I engage in, reminds me of my purpose—to love and to serve. Inner peace is not simply about my connection to God; it is about miraculous transformations ignited by that connection. It's an invitation to allow God's love to flow through me into the lives of others."

In Christianity, the call to serve is equally potent. The teachings of Jesus highlight the importance of loving one's neighbour as oneself, and this message is echoed through numerous mystic traditions. Many mystics integrate acts of kindness as an essential part of their spiritual practice, believing that such actions are not only expressions of faith but bridges connecting all of humanity.

Through individual testimonies, it becomes clear that spirituality functions as a lifelong journey of learning and growth. The Harmoniser emphasises that what unites Christians and Muslims is not only a desire for spiritual fulfilment but a shared mission to cultivate peace, love, and mutual respect in a discordant world.

The exploration of Sufism and Mystical Theology reveals the layers of spirituality embedded within each faith. Both traditions offer rich avenues for followers to navigate their innermost thoughts, seeking guidance and peace that surpass understanding. Personal stories flow like rivers, carving pathways through the rocky landscapes of doubt and uncertainty, illuminating the divine truth that both God and humanity desire a close connection.

The Harmoniser invites readers to reflect on their spiritual journeys, recognising that every soul is on a unique path as they explore the intersections of mysticism, love, and the pursuit of peace. The wonders of spirituality unfold, revealing a profound kinship in belief and experience.

In drawing this exploration to a close, it is essential to acknowledge the transformative power of spirituality. As adherents of both Christianity and Islam engage with their spiritual practices, they embark on a journey of becoming—their hearts expanding with love, their minds opening to understanding, and their souls yearning for a deeper communion with God.

In essence, spirituality invites believers to move beyond the confines of rituals and doctrines, encouraging a profoundly intimate and universally connective personal exploration of the Divine. The Harmoniser's reflections resonate powerfully through this narrative, urging all who are on this journey to embrace spirituality as a means to cultivate not only an inner sanctuary of peace but also a collective mission to foster understanding and compassion in a world yearning for healing.

The Practice of Charity

In the heart of both Christianity and Islam lies an essential tenet that transcends the mere act of giving: charity. This principle, deeply embedded within the doctrinal frameworks of both faiths, underscores the moral obligation believers have towards one another and the wider community. Charity in Christianity, often expressed through the practice of Tithing, and the Islamic concept of Zakat emphasises the significance of generosity as an expression of faith, demonstrating devotion, and adherence to the teachings of their respective scriptures.

At its core, charity is not merely a philanthropic gesture; it is an act of spiritual substance that reflects a believer's faith and connection to the Divine. It serves as a bridge between the spiritual and the tangible, a way to materialise one's love and compassion towards others while reinforcing the sense of community that both religions promote. This subchapter will delve into the significance of charity in both faiths, showcasing personal stories of transformation and community service that illuminate the profound impact of these practices.

Zakat, meaning purification, is often defined as a mandatory form of almsgiving in Islam, representing one of the Five Pillars that form the foundation of Muslim life. The word itself means to purify, implying that by giving part of one's wealth, a believer purifies their remaining possessions and soul. For many Muslims, practising Zakat is not merely an obligation but a privilege to aid those less fortunate. The Quran emphasises this notion, asserting that wealth is a trust from God, and it is to be shared. In Surah Al-Baqarah, believers are reminded, "And establish prayer and give Zakat and obey the Messenger - that you may receive mercy."

One of the remarkable aspects of Zakat is its structured approach to wealth distribution. Typically, Muslims are required to give 2.5% of their savings and assets annually, which is sufficient to make a real difference in the lives of those in need. This obligation prompts believers to be aware of their financial situations and encourages a sense of accountability. Far from being a tedious obligation, enabling fellow human beings to rise from poverty or face challenges becomes a source of spiritual fulfilment.

Across the globe, Muslims are known to fulfil this obligation, transforming lives through the provision of educational opportunities, healthcare, and emergency relief. One poignant example comes from a small village in Bangladesh, where a teacher had devoted her life to educating young girls in the community, facing significant financial barriers. Through the Zakat contributions she and others received, the teacher was able to establish a scholarship fund, enabling numerous girls to attend school and leading to unprecedented improvements in literacy and empowerment within the village. This initiative, born out of the religious obligation of charity, opened doors to opportunity and change that would ripple through generations.

While Zakat is a structured practice, charity within Christianity often evolves from a more personalised approach. Tithing refers to the practice of donating a portion, traditionally one-tenth, of one's income to the church or for charitable purposes. Rooted in biblical teachings, Tithing finds its origins in the Old Testament, where individuals were encouraged to bring the first fruits of their harvests as a sign of gratitude and as an act of worship. In **Deuteronomy 14:22-29**, the implications of this practice extend beyond personal spirituality, inviting believers to foster their community's growth by supporting those in need within their midst.

This multifaceted approach towards charity, exemplified in the parable of the Good Samaritan, illustrates the Christian understanding of neighbourly love. The narrative depicts an individual who, despite societal divides and expectations, took it upon himself to assist a battered stranger—a strong testament to the spontaneity of Christian charity. It encapsulates how acts of kindness transcend formal obligations, reflective of one's love for God, manifested through love for others.

In contemporary society, Tithing remains a vital aspect of church life for many Christians and has been pronounced an act of faith and devotion. Churches employ Tithing as a means to support their missions, provide social assistance, or help fund outreach programs. Communities that integrate systematic charitable giving often witness positive transformations.

One such instance is found in a local parish where church members began a Tithing initiative collected through their weekly services. Funds collected not only sustained church operations but also empowered the congregation to launch community outreach programs such as food banks and shelters for the homeless. Stories emerged of lives transformed, families fed, and hope restored, serving as vivid reminders that the act of giving is intertwined with love, compassion, and communal responsibility.

While Tithing represents a structured form of giving, everyday acts of kindness, informal donations, and engagement in community service also hold significant importance in Christian teaching. Volunteers at food banks or shelters are engaging in a practice that mirrors scriptural mandates, fostering a spirit of generosity as they serve. Whether it is a simple gesture, such as sharing a meal or contributing to disaster relief funds, Christians embody their faith by committing themselves to acts of service and charity.

Across religious lines, numerous initiatives have sprung from the shared ethos around charity between Muslims and Christians. In many communities worldwide, both faiths come together to address pressing social issues, such as homelessness and hunger, while advocating for social justice. One inspiring example emerges from Detroit, where a coalition of Christian and Muslim organisations came together in an effort to address food insecurity. They formed community gardens, shared resources, and together mobilised volunteers to raise awareness and distribute food to families in need. What started as a dire response grew into lasting alliances rooted in a mutual commitment to serve, illustrating how shared personal beliefs could kindle the spirit of unity.

Despite their differences, at the heart of both faiths lies the realisation that charity is a catalyst for social change, not only alleviating suffering but also strengthening community bonds. Individuals who embrace their responsibility to help others often find their lives enriched with purpose and meaning. Stories emerge, painting the rich tapestry of humanity transformed through acts of kindness.

Consider the story of Fatima, a young Muslim woman whose family struggled with financial hardship after her father fell ill. Through the generosity of community members who contributed Zakat, Fatima was able not only to pursue higher education but also to advocate for others facing similar crises. Embracing the cycle of giving she experienced firsthand, Fatima initiated a student organisation dedicated to supporting low-income families within her university. By fostering an ethos of giving amongst her peers, she demonstrated how acts of charity can transcend immediate needs, nurturing long-term commitments to service.

Similarly, Chris, a devoted Christian, found his calling through modern-day challenges and the enthusiasm of his youth group. After engaging in volunteer work at a homeless shelter and observing the impact of Tithing, he was inspired to develop an initiative where church members could work with local businesses to collect donations. Chris recalls, "Every week we met, and our combined efforts meant we were able to serve over two hundred people monthly. When you experience the difference you can make together, it's hard to turn back—this is how faith leads us!"

Christianity and Islam - Two paths, One Purpose

The interconnected nature of charity reflects more than compliance with religious doctrines; it illustrates the innate desire to cultivate goodness within society. Acts of charity intertwine with profound personal transformation, illuminating lives and serving as pathways to understanding that promote unity among religious communities.

Compassion through charity can further extend to social activism, as individuals mobilise to address systemic injustices and poverty. The Sadaqah, a voluntary form of charity in Islam, and many forms of charitable acts taken by Christians echo the dedication of individuals to advocate for policies that resonate with their beliefs. Charity becomes a means of bridging divides, empowering individuals to confront injustices, and ensuring that marginalised voices are heard in the fabric of humanitarian concerns.

As philanthropy continues to evolve, charitable foundations are springing from within both faith communities, further amplifying the reach of philanthropic activities. Several organisations dedicated to uplifting communities in need emerge, seeking to inspire both Muslims and Christians to collaborate on projects that serve the common good.

In the effort to tackle poverty and homelessness, for instance, interfaith organisations have become instrumental in promoting understanding and service. Globally, the trend toward greater collaboration between diverse faith groups showcases a collective commitment towards charity, and the practice is further amplified when believers work side by side for social change. It illustrates the broader concept that faith, when interwoven, can create ripples of hope, regardless of one's religious background.

Moreover, the experiences derived from charitable acts weave the individual into the larger narrative of community and faith. Personal stories of challenges and triumphs provide rich illustrations of how charity transcends mere obligation, fostering a culture of giving that feels like an integral part of a believer's journey. The commitment to serve through acts of charity reinforces the idea that giving not only enriches the lives of others but also enriches the giver.

Leverage this wisdom through narratives of resilience and determination that lie among both communities. The rich stories of people taking concrete actions to embrace the spirit of charity help form the heart of these faith traditions. Building a foundation for deeper connections, one that transcends religious boundaries and is rooted in a shared understanding of humanity, brings us to the next chapter in our collective journey toward hope and social justice.

In conclusion, this exploration of charity within Christianity and Islam demonstrates that, beyond being an obligation, it serves as a pathway toward forming deep connections among individuals and communities. Whether through Zakat, Tithing, or any form of charitable acts, believers arrive at a common understanding that generosity emerges as a defining characteristic of faith, manifested through care and compassion for one another.

We must continue to recognise the transformative power of such practices, nurturing both individual growth and communal bonds. As these narratives of giving unravel within the contemplative hearts of believers, both Islam and Christianity not only come closer to embodying their ethical teachings but also pave the way for unity, understanding, and love—a gift worthy of being shared.

Faith in Dialogue: A Timeless Exchange

Historical Interactions and Exchanges

The interactions between Christians and Muslims throughout history have been as complex as they are profound. From peaceful collaboration to intense conflict, the relationship between these two faiths has shaped societies, influenced cultures, and forged resilient bonds that persist today. This subchapter delves into the pivotal moments of contact, change, and coexistence, tracing their historical pathways that enrich the narratives of both religions and emphasising the intricate dialogues that emerge from their shared histories.

The earliest significant interactions can be traced back to the early days of Islam in the 7th century. The life of the Prophet Muhammad marked the beginning of the Islamic tradition, and it was during this formative period that relations with the Christian community began to be established. While the Arabian Peninsula was home to many religious traditions, including various forms of monotheism, Christians inhabited adjacent regions from the Byzantine Empire to the Arabian frontier. A combination of trade, dialogue, and theological disputes shaped the encounters between Muslims and Christians during these initial years. These exchanges would lay the groundwork for future interactions and set the stage for both cooperation and conflict.

As Islam spread rapidly across the Arabian Peninsula and beyond, the early Muslim community primarily engaged with its Christian counterparts through trade and diplomacy. The Treaty of Hudaybiyyah, signed in 628 CE, established an armistice between Muhammad's followers and the Quraysh tribe, illustrating the significance of peaceful coexistence. Even as Christianity was dominant within the declining Roman Empire, the growing Islamic influence required that Muslims and Christians navigate their interactions with finesse, acknowledging their profound theological differences while also respecting each other's beliefs.

The Golden Age of Islam, spanning from the 8th to the 14th centuries, serves as a period of remarkable intellectual exchange between Muslims and Christians. This era is characterised by an environment that fosters collaboration between scholars of both faiths, particularly in regions such as Al-Andalus (modern-day Spain), where cultures intertwined, leading to the flourishing of centres of learning. The city of Córdoba emerged as a beacon of knowledge, where Christian, Muslim, and Jewish scholars converged to share ideas in mathematics, astronomy, medicine, and philosophy.

In this vibrant environment, significant figures such as Averroes (Ibn Rushd), a Muslim philosopher, played a key role in bridging the intellectual traditions of Christianity and Islam. Averroes's commentaries on Aristotle challenged theological frameworks and initiated discussions that would resonate in the medieval universities of Europe. These scholarly pursuits were not confined solely to philosophical discourse; they touched upon the very essence of faith and existence, revealing how both traditions sought understanding through their interpretations of life, the universe, and the divine.

In a striking illustration of this collaborative spirit, the Christian polymath and translator, Gerard of Cremona, relocated to Toledo, where he transformed Arabic texts into Latin, thereby transmitting critical knowledge to the Christian world. This translation movement not only preserved ancient wisdom but also introduced innovative concepts that advanced European thought. The mutual humility displayed by both Christian and Muslim scholars in the pursuit of truth paved the way for resonant ideas, forging connections that transcended their theological divisions.

However, as the intellectual exchanges thrived, tensions simmered beneath the surface. The Reconquista, the centuries-long campaign by Christian kingdoms to reclaim territories occupied by Muslims in the Iberian Peninsula, marked a significant turning point in relations. Hostilities ignited as Christian leaders viewed the Islamic presence as a threat and pursued policies of reconquest. The Crusades, commencing in the late 11th century, epitomised this era of conflict, as armies from Europe launched military campaigns to reclaim the Holy Land.

The Crusades not only represent a historical confrontation but also elucidate the deep entanglement between faith and identity. In the fervour of these campaigns, ideology intertwined with the aspirations of power led to devastating consequences for both sides. The seemingly insurmountable divide compelled communities to reassess their perceptions of one another. Yet, amidst the chaos, notable exchanges occurred, as merchants traded goods, ideas, and knowledge even during wartime. The Crusaders, while initially motivated by the desire for conquest, often found themselves navigating a culturally rich and vastly different world—a world shaped by the very faith they sought to challenge.

The encounters during the Crusades instigated a cycle of mutual animosity, but they also fostered familiarity with cultural gifts. Christian pilgrims returning from the East brought back intricacies of Islamic architecture, science, and philosophy that profoundly influenced European thought. Gothic cathedrals were infused with elements of Islamic art, and the study of mathematics—bolstered by the numerals introduced from the Islamic world—revolutionised European scientific approaches. Thus, even amid discord, a thread of exchange pulsed through the cultural landscape, uniting the two faiths in unexpected ways.

As the Middle Ages wore on, the interactions continued to evolve. The Ottoman Empire, which expanded its reach into Southeast Europe, played a crucial role in reshaping the dynamics among Christians and Muslims. The coexistence of vastly diverse populations under Ottoman rule fostered environments where interfaith dialogues flourished. This period witnessed the emergence of communities that blended customs, languages, and traditions from both religions, creating layered identities that drew from their shared legacies.

In places like Istanbul, formerly Constantinople, the integration of Christian and Muslim practices became a symbol of this coexistence. Churches were transformed into mosques and vice versa, symbolising not only the cultural amalgamation but also a testament to the resilience of faith amid changing power structures. The notion of 'millet' allowed religious communities to maintain their distinct practices while operating under a broader Ottoman identity, enabling varying interpretations of faith to thrive alongside one another.

Despite periods of cooperation, tensions persisted, particularly during the rise of nationalism in the 19th and early 20th centuries. The decline of empires often led to shifting alliances and increased divisions, as political aspirations infiltrated religious identities. The legacy of colonialism exacerbated these fissures, as Western imperial powers exerted influence over Muslim-majority countries.

Christianity and Islam - Two paths, One Purpose

In this context, religious identities were often entangled in the politics of power, leading to new rounds of animosity that would resonate into contemporary times.

The historical interactions culminate in the ongoing dialogues that emerge in today's world. Understanding the complexities of Christian-Muslim relations requires acknowledging both the struggles and collaborations that have defined their shared history. Scholars such as Karen Armstrong and John L. Esposito emphasise the importance of rediscovering the historical threads of dialogue, demonstrating how encounters during the Golden Age and the tensions of the Crusades continue to resonate in current interfaith discussions.

In the landscape of modernity, the legacy of these historical exchanges shapes contemporary relationships as communities seek paths toward reconciliation. Interfaith dialogue initiatives, developed in response to past hostilities, aim to build bridges of understanding and foster cooperation among varying beliefs. These dialogues echo the very spirit of collaboration that characterised the Golden Age—a time when ideas transcended borders, when scholars from myriad backgrounds came together to pursue knowledge.

Today, as societies grapple with the challenges of globalisation and extremism, the stories of cooperation and cultural exchange offer crucial insights. An understanding of our shared past can illuminate pathways toward a future characterised by respect and collaboration. The work of community leaders and activists striving for social justice highlights how individuals from both faith traditions come together to address common challenges, reinforcing the notion that despite historical conflicts, the potential for partnership remains strong.

As we navigate the present, the ongoing dialogue enriched by history serves as a reminder that the intersection of faith can yield remarkable outcomes. Recognition of shared values, mutual respect, and the celebration of diversity are essential in shaping a more harmonious coexistence. The historical interactions between Christians and Muslims inform contemporary conversations, offering valuable lessons that transcend the confines of religious differences.

As interfaith initiatives continue to emerge globally, they foster spaces where followers of both faiths come together for understanding and cooperation, echoing the scholarly exchanges of the Golden Age. The timeless pursuit of knowledge, compassion, and justice, rooted in the intertwined narratives of Christianity and Islam, provides fertile ground for collaborative actions today.

In conclusion, the historical tapestry woven by the interactions between Christians and Muslims presents a narrative marked by both conflict and cooperation. The legacy of these encounters shapes the present dialogue, reminding us of our shared humanity and the need for understanding in the face of diversity. It is through acknowledging our historical entanglements that we can aspire to foster a future in which peace and respect guide our relationships, transcending the boundaries of faith to unite in our common quest for knowledge, justice, and mutual respect.

Conversations of Faith

In a world increasingly marked by division, the conversations of faith have emerged as vital bridges, fostering understanding and respect between diverse communities. The dialogues that take place between religious leaders and laypersons alike illuminate both the best of human nature and the profound desire for connection across differing beliefs. This subchapter aims to examine contemporary interfaith initiatives that foster collaborative solutions to pressing societal challenges, promoting mutual understanding between Christian and Muslim communities.

To understand the landscape of interfaith dialogue today, it is essential to start by recognising the voices that are leading these discussions. Over the past few decades, numerous organisations and leaders have committed themselves to the task of nurturing relationships among faith communities, advocating for a spirit of cooperation rather than conflict. Their stories and insights provide a rich background against which contemporary interfaith initiatives can be examined.

One such leader is Dr. Sayyid Muhammad Rizvi, an influential Shia Muslim scholar and the Imam of the Islamic Institute of Toronto. Dr. Rizvi's work exemplifies the potential for dialogue between faiths, especially in multicultural contexts. His advocacy for understanding and respect leads to productive conversations about shared ethics and values. In a recent interview, Dr. Rizvi shared that he was inspired to engage in interfaith dialogue after witnessing the devastating impacts of misinformation and stereotypes during heightened political tensions.

"I believe it is our responsibility, as faith leaders, to create spaces where our communities can engage with each other meaningfully," he stated. "The more we understand one another's beliefs and practices, the fewer the misconceptions, and the more we can work together towards a common good."

These ideals are echoed by Father Michael Lapsley, an Anglican priest and founder of the Institute for Healing of Memories in South

Africa. Father Lapsley, who lost both hands in a letter bomb explosion during apartheid, emphasises forgiveness and reconciliation as essential elements in faith dialogue. He passionately stated:

"Interfaith dialogue is not just about understanding differences; it's about healing the wounds of division and moving forward together. When we share our stories—our struggles, our hopes—we walk the path of healing that our communities desperately need."

Father Lapsley's experiences in conflict resolution have shown him firsthand how conversations of faith can lead to transformative outcomes. At the Institute for Healing of Memories, he facilitates workshops where individuals from various faith backgrounds come together to share their narratives, fostering empathy and advocating for social justice. The methodology has proven successful in post-conflict scenarios, providing participants with tools for reconciliation while promoting interfaith unity.

Examining these narratives underscores the role of interfaith dialogue as a catalyst for change. Many communities are now engaging in joint service projects that address social challenges such as poverty, education, and healthcare. These initiatives not only provide tangible assistance but also help to form lasting relationships among diverse faith groups.

One notable program is the Unity in Diversity initiative, which brings together Christian and Muslim volunteers to work on community service projects in urban areas. Established in response to neighbourhoods experiencing tension, the program has focused efforts on food security and youth mentorship.

Christianity and Islam - Two paths, One Purpose

During a recent community event, the participants shared their experiences of collaborating side by side in feeding projects. Fatima, a young Muslim volunteer, exclaimed:

"Working with my Christian friends on these projects has opened my eyes to how much we can achieve together. We may come from different perspectives, but we all want the same things for our community—peace, love, and understanding."

John, a Christian mentor, affirmed Fatima's sentiment by reflecting on their interactions:

"The conversations we have are often more powerful than the tasks we complete. We learn from one another's traditions and values, and it's a beautiful reminder of what unity can look like."

This testimonial underscores how interfaith dialogues forge connections that transcend profound differences. The opportunity to engage in shared activities reinforces community bonds and counters stereotypes that often persist in ignorance.

A significant challenge for many interfaith dialogues today is the backdrop of political tensions and global conflicts fueled by misunderstanding and fear. Recognising the current challenges is essential to navigating these conversations effectively. The rise of extremist groups that manipulate faith narratives has created barriers to understanding, making the role of dialogue even more critical.

Rabbi Daniel Weiner, a leader in interfaith initiatives, articulates the situation succinctly: "We must confront our own biases and educate ourselves, not only about our traditions but also about the beliefs of others. Equipping ourselves with knowledge will pave the way for richer discussions and fruitful encounters."

Christianity and Islam - Two paths, One Purpose

In his work with the Greater Boston Interfaith Organisation, Rabbi Weiner has engaged interfaith partners in a range of projects focused on social justice, including advocating for affordable housing and combating hate crimes. By addressing these pressing issues through collaborative efforts, faith leaders are demonstrating that their convictions extend beyond religious ceremonies to encompass genuine concern for the welfare of society.

Learning from these examples also means recognising the significance of youth in interfaith dialogue. Younger generations are increasingly taking the helm, advocating for inclusivity and understanding in ways that resonate with their peers. Initiatives that target youth involvement create vibrant spaces for collaboration, where social media plays a crucial role in disseminating information and fostering connectivity.

One inspiring instance involves the Youth Interfaith Network, a grassroots organisation created by students from various backgrounds. They convene regularly for discussions, workshops, and community outreach programs, seeking to foster friendships across faiths while addressing challenges unique to youth today, such as mental health and social justice.

During a meeting with the network, Mariam, a Muslim participant, expressed her aspirations:

"With everything we face today, I feel we must break down walls and build bridges. This is our chance to show that we can come together, with our different experiences, and create something powerful."

John, a Christian member, echoed this optimism, stating:

"Youth have the power to lead the change we want to see. If we can unite in our efforts and share our stories, we can inspire those around us to do the same."

The authenticity and passion that emerge from youth-focused interfaith dialogues serve as a source of hope. They remind us that the future of faith-based collaboration lies in engaging the emerging generations, providing them with the tools to navigate complexities while forging relationships that transcend inherent differences.

One practical example of success in interfaith dialogue is the annual Interfaith Harmony Week, celebrated globally, which invites communities to organise events and activities that promote harmony among people of different faiths. By showcasing local efforts, communities share their successes and inspire others, stimulating a collective effort toward reconciliation and goodwill.

Participants across various events have engaged in meaningful conversations that reinforce shared values, whether through shared meals, artistic expressions, or community service. Each event sends a powerful message reflecting a commitment to peace and understanding.

Furthermore, organisations like the World Faiths Development Dialogue focus on leveraging the resources of faith communities to tackle pressing global issues, such as poverty and inequality. This collaboration highlights how faith-based perspectives can significantly enrich approaches to development, promising not only material outcomes but also fostering a sense of belonging and interconnectedness among diverse groups.

As these initiatives thrive, it remains crucial to assess their impact and sustainability. Conversations of faith should not be fleeting encounters but rather become ingrained in the fabric of communities. Lasting results emerge when dialogue is embedded within broader organisational frameworks that address ongoing relationships and pave the way for future collaboration.

Finding ways to measure the success of interfaith dialogues offers insights into their effectiveness. Feedback from participants, changes in community dynamics, and newfound partnerships are tangible indicators that serve as benchmarks for growth. Additionally, sharing outcomes through storytelling amplifies awareness and encourages others to participate.

To navigate the future, faith leaders must collaborate closely with community activists, educators, and policymakers. By creating inclusive platforms for knowledge-sharing and collaboration, they can reinforce common ground while continuing to engage with divergent views. This collaborative storytelling can rewrite narratives, transforming misunderstandings into compassionate engagements.

Nevertheless, the journey of interfaith dialogue is neither simple nor linear. The path is often fraught with challenges, requiring patience and courage from all involved. Leaders must engage earnestly with their constituents, addressing suspicions and discomfort while steadily building trust. It is an investment in the future—one that recognises the power of listening and learning.

As we reflect on the lessons learned through these dialogues, the goal extends beyond coexistence; a more profound aspiration lies in cultivating friendships that inspire collective action for a better world. These friendships create ripples of change, inviting more stakeholders into discussions and championing the potential for grassroots movements.

Ultimately, the conversations of faith are not solely academic or theoretical pursuits; they emerge from lived experiences and personal struggles. By shedding light on the need for dialogue, we can celebrate our differences and foster an understanding that propels social justice and collective growth. Through these efforts, we strive to build a legacy not only on the recognition of shared beliefs but also on collaborative action that drives humanity forward.

The ongoing dialogues that span cultures and religions stand as testaments to humanity's resilience and ability to form connections amidst adversity. The stories of those engaged in interfaith initiatives underscore the richness of diversity and the pathways that lead to greater understanding. In doing so, they illuminate the potential for faith to unite rather than divide, laying the groundwork for a harmonious future marked by compassion, collaboration, and peace.

As we close this exploration of contemporary interfaith dialogues, it is essential to consider not only the challenges but also the immense opportunities that lie ahead. The threads of connection we weave today through conversations of faith have the power to create a tapestry of harmony, illustrating that while we may walk different paths, we are united in our pursuit of understanding and respect.

The Role of Community Engagement

In an increasingly diverse and interconnected world, the role of community engagement among faith communities assumes profound importance. This subchapter examines grassroots movements where Christians and Muslims unite for social justice, showcasing how faith-driven individuals collaborate to address societal challenges. Through various initiatives, from food drives to peace marches, we will uncover the transformative impact of unity in action.

As we reflect on personal experiences and stories from those who have witnessed the power of collaboration, it becomes clear that these interactions not only enhance understanding but also inspire hope. The Discoverer, tasked with sharing these narratives, reminds us that our collective journey towards justice and equity is rooted in shared values, drawing deeply from the moral foundations laid by both Christianity and Islam.

The first story we encounter is set in a bustling urban neighbourhood, where a local church and mosque have forged a partnership to address food insecurity. What started as a small community concern escalated into a broader initiative involving both faith communities. The Discoverer recalls the inaugural food drive, filled with anticipation and hope, as members from both faiths gathered at the community centre.

In this vibrant setting, tables were laden with fresh produce, canned goods, and essentials. Volunteers from both the church and mosque worked side by side, sorting through donations, sharing laughs, and exchanging life stories. This act of sharing resources transcended mere charity; it cultivated relationships, fostering a deeper understanding of one another's traditions and values.

"Seeing the joy on people's faces as they left with bags of groceries was indescribable," the Discoverer reflects. "It was about more than just feeding the hungry; it was about witnessing the very essence of community." This particular food drive grew from a one-time event into a monthly occurrence, illustrating how grassroots movements can grow organically with dedication and collaboration.

Christianity and Islam - Two paths, One Purpose

In the months that followed, the Discoverer observed how this initiative not only tackled food insecurity but also became a platform for dialogue. Community meetings were organised, encouraging participants to share their insights on societal issues and potential solutions. As they gathered, faith communities exchanged ideas on how to address the systematic undercurrents of poverty, demonstrating a commitment to social justice rooted in their mutual beliefs.

One of the most powerful moments occurred when community members decided to host an interfaith festival to celebrate their collaborative efforts. The festival was a tapestry of cultural expressions, featuring food, music, and storytelling from both traditions. It was here that families from diverse backgrounds mingled, creating an atmosphere of unity and celebration.

"Watching children laugh and play together, oblivious to the divides that often separate adults, was a sight to behold," the Discoverer notes. "These acts of engagement not only promote understanding but dismantle barriers built on misconceptions." The success of the festival signified that faith can indeed be a catalyst for positive change.

As active neighbours in their community, these individuals were not just addressing immediate needs; they were becoming advocates for broader reforms. The Discoverer witnessed how various discussions from these community gatherings led to a campaign advocating for affordable housing, access to education, and more equitable employment opportunities.

Inspired by their solidarity, the church and mosque leaders came together to draft a community manifesto that outlined their commitment to social justice. This document served as a guiding light, urging members to take action and engage in public discourse. Through it, they reaffirmed their shared commitment to promoting dignity, justice, and compassion for all individuals.

One poignant episode in this journey occurred during a local council meeting, where a proposed policy was addressed that could potentially disenfranchise many residents. Representatives from both communities stood together to voice their concerns, exemplifying how two faith groups united in purpose can amplify their impact. The Discoverer recalls the palpable energy in that room as both Christians and Muslims found common ground in advocating for the marginalised.

The lessons learned in this grassroots initiative did not remain isolated. Similar projects began sprouting up in neighbouring towns, inspired by the collaborative spirit fostered through these interfaith dialogues. The Discoverer observed this ripple effect, where one act of unity sparked multiple movements, creating a network of support across communities.

The story of the food drive and interfaith festival highlights a powerful truth: when individuals of different faiths come together for a common cause, they create bridges that connect them and to broader societal needs. The Discoverer muses, "These connections foster empathy, allowing us to learn from one another and walk alongside each other in our struggles."

Yet, community engagement is not without its challenges. Throughout this journey, the Discoverer also witnessed moments of tension and misunderstanding. There were instances when individuals from either faith community felt uncertain about working with the other due to preconceived notions or stereotypes. The leaders needed to address these concerns head-on.

Facilitated dialogue sessions became instrumental in navigating these complexities. These gatherings often included reflective exercises, encouraging participants to share their experiences and openly discuss their fears. One night, during one of these dialogues, an elder from the mosque spoke passionately about his experiences growing up in a community that was not always welcoming to those different from them, recounting tales of prejudice and resilience.

Another participant, a church member, shared her own story of displacement and the isolation that comes with being viewed as 'the other.' Through these exchanges, empathy blossomed, enabling both groups to understand each other's backgrounds better and, in the process, heal old wounds.

"Confronting these challenges was difficult but necessary," the Discoverer states. "True community engagement requires vulnerability and honesty about our fears, histories, and misconceptions." This understanding laid the groundwork for deeper relationships, reinforcing the idea that every individual, regardless of their faith, holds valuable experiences that enrich the collective narrative.

As community engagement continued to grow, initiatives like community service projects, educational programs, and youth activities emerged, amplifying the impact of their collaboration. Young people from both communities were encouraged to take active roles in these initiatives, recognising the potential for the next generation to cultivate understanding and change at an earlier stage.

One initiative born from this collaboration was a mentorship program that paired Muslim and Christian youths, allowing them to learn from each other's experiences and perspectives. The Discoverer recalls a poignant moment from a gathering where a young Christian boy spoke about his dreams of becoming a doctor. At the same time, his Muslim counterpart expressed a desire to become an engineer. Their aspirations led to discussions about the importance of education, culminating in joint study sessions and projects that promoted academic excellence.

The mentorship program flourished, leading to the establishment of a youth council that fostered interfaith dialogue and community service. Participants organised clean-up days in their neighbourhoods, collected supplies for shelters, and volunteered at community centres. Through these hands-on experiences, the youth discovered their shared value of service, reinforcing their commitment to standing together against injustice.

As they engaged with their community, these young people became ambassadors of unity, reminding adults of the power and transformative potential of collaborative, faith-driven efforts. They coined the phrase "One Community, Many Faiths" as a rallying cry, emblematic of their collective efforts to promote understanding and connection.

Reflecting on these youth-led initiatives, the Discoverer emphasises the importance of mentorship from seasoned leaders while allowing young voices to flourish. Youth leadership has proven essential in reshaping narratives and breaking down barriers, reminding everyone of the inherent strength that comes from diversity.

Community engagement, at its heart, is a continuous journey. As both faith communities worked alongside one another, they faced the unfolding realities of society, fighting for justice in various forms. From advocating against discrimination to addressing climate change, the initiatives undertaken bore witness to the ever-changing landscape of community needs.

A profound example emerged when social justice movements gained momentum. As protests swept across various cities demanding change, leaders from both communities came together to organise a peaceful march centred on equality and justice. Drawing from the shared values outlined in their respective scriptures, they framed their efforts within the teachings of their faiths that call upon adherents to stand against oppression.

The atmosphere was electric as Christians and Muslims joined hands and walked side by side. The Discoverer recalls the chants that filled the air, echoing the desire for justice and equity. "The sight of diverse individuals united in purpose was a testament to what we can achieve when we let go of our differences and focus on our common goals," he says, overwhelmed by the overwhelming feeling of solidarity.

Throughout the march, stories circulated of individuals who had once harboured doubts, finding their perspectives transformed as they participated. New friendships blossomed, built on shared experiences and mutual understanding. After the march, forums were held to reflect on their experiences, allowing participants to express how this collaboration had shifted their perceptions of one another.

The Discoverer found himself reflective of the journey thus far. "Community engagement challenges us to confront our own biases while enriching our perspectives," he shared. "Amidst the challenges and triumphs, we witness the undeniable truth that we are better together."

The stories emerging from grassroots community engagement movements highlight the manifold ways faith communities can join forces in pursuit of a common good. By recognising shared values and ideals, Christians and Muslims have demonstrated that collaboration can transcend barriers that might otherwise divide them. This powerful example of unity illustrates that faith-driven social justice efforts are not only meaningful but necessary in our complex world.

As we conclude this exploration into the role of community engagement, it is clear that the endeavours of these individuals have laid a foundation for future interactions. The Discoverer recognises these grassroots initiatives as a starting point for broader dialogues, emphasising the importance of nurturing relationships that can withstand the test of time.

Indeed, the journey of community engagement continues, propelled by passion, purpose, and unity in action. As individuals, the faithful are called to embrace understanding, recognise shared experiences, and celebrate their collective humanity. In doing so, they cultivate an environment where love, respect, and compassion reign, illustrating the powerful role faith can play in fostering a more just and equitable world.

Modern Reflections: The State of Faith Today

Challenges of Misunderstanding

In a world characterised by rapid globalisation and interconnectivity, the religious landscape has found itself both challenged and enriched by the currents of misunderstanding. The subchapter "Challenges of Misunderstanding" aims to dissect these misconceptions, particularly between Christianity and Islam, and to illustrate how these misunderstandings breed conflict and division, while simultaneously advocating for empathy and clarity.

Misunderstandings between followers of different religions often originate in stereotypes—generalisations that oversimplify and distort the realities of individual beliefs and practices. In many cases, media portrayals serve to reinforce these stereotypes, painting broad strokes over complex narratives. For instance, following global conflicts or terrorist attacks, news outlets may emphasise the religious affiliations of perpetrators, leading to sweeping judgments that implicate entire communities. These portrayals can perpetuate a toxic cycle where individuals define one another not by their character, but by a singular or violent action that misrepresents the values held by the majority.

One poignant example is the perception of Muslims post-9/11. Many were vilified as extremists due to the heinous actions of a small group. This stereotype escalated into a broader societal misconception that Islam itself was a violent religion. Conversations with practitioners reveal the profound sadness and frustration inherent in this characterisation. Fatima, a young Muslim woman from New York, shared:

"Every time I hear someone say 'Muslims are terrorists,' it feels like a personal attack on my faith and my family. I want people to see that our teachings encourage peace, compassion, and community. Yet, the narrative seems to overshadow the kindness that permeates our actions."

This sentiment reflects a shared burden felt by many communities, particularly those who find themselves on the periphery of public scrutiny. According to John, a devout Christian living in a multicultural neighbourhood,

"The media doesn't help. Whenever there's bad news involving Muslims, it's as if the entire faith is put on trial. Few stories of interfaith collaboration make headlines, and it creates an environment of mistrust and fear. I've seen it firsthand; once, I organised an event inviting local Muslims to discuss our differences, but the turnout was less than what I hoped because people were afraid to engage."

The political landscape often exacerbates these misunderstandings. The rhetoric employed by political leaders can fortify binary oppositions—us versus them—that fuel divisions among communities. The portrayal of Muslims in legislative discussions around immigration and national security exemplifies this dynamic. Profiling Muslims as suspects in potential terror plots, without recognising their contributions to society, reduces a diverse populace to a singular, dangerous identity.

One major misconception that echoes within political discourse is the idea that advocating for rights or safety for Muslim communities equates to compromising the values of Christianity or Western ideals. This false dichotomy not only vilifies Muslims but also creates a rift within the Christian community. Sister Mary, a nun dedicated to social justice, expressed her thoughts candidly:

"As a Christian, it pains me to see how our faith is warped in the political arena. We're called to love our neighbours, yet so many ignore that command in favour of fear. People forget that our teachings are about uplifting the oppressed, not fearing them. Diversity should enrich our faith, not dilute it."

The intersection of media portrayals and political rhetoric fosters an environment where misunderstandings flourish, overshadowing nuanced conversations about faith. Nevertheless, it is crucial to present the experiences of individuals who have taken steps to bridge these divides. Stories of collaboration can illuminate how Christians and Muslims work together for common causes, combating myths with shared experiences.

Consider the narrative of the Interfaith Alliance, an organisation that convenes individuals from various faith backgrounds to address social justice issues. Their annual forum attracts participants from both Muslim and Christian communities, creating spaces that encourage dialogue rather than division. Ahmed, a member of the alliance, shared,

"At our last meeting, we talked about food insecurity. The assumption was that we couldn't work together, but with shared values of compassion at heart, we found ways to collaborate on initiatives, such as food drives. When you're working side by side for a common cause, those misconceptions fade away."

Personal stories, such as those from Ahmed and Sister Mary, exemplify a broader trend of interfaith collaboration that strives to dismantle the walls built by misunderstanding. However, these efforts often go unnoticed in mainstream discussions about religion, overshadowed by narratives steeped in conflict.

The challenge remains not only in fostering these collaborations but also in encouraging individuals to share their stories more openly. The voices seeking clarity amid confusion need to be amplified, reminding communities of the fundamental teachings at the heart of both Christianity and Islam: love, mercy, and justice. These are common threads woven through the moral fabric of both religions, yet often they get lost in translation, wrapped in fear-driven rhetoric.

The stories of individuals coming to understand one another are crucial in redefining the narrative. Lamia, a Muslim mother whose children play with their Christian neighbours, shared,

"We often hold potlucks together. The joy comes not just from the food but from breaking bread with those we might've hesitated to engage with in the past. Our kids grow up seeing us laugh together, showing them that our differences make each other richer, not poorer.

These stories emphasise the real, everyday actions that counterbalance the prevalent misunderstandings. They highlight how personal connections can provide colour to black-and-white portrayals of faith, reflecting the beauty found in coexistence. For individuals willing to take the step toward mutual understanding, the rewards can be profound.

Moreover, understanding the role of education in misperceptions can prove valuable in dismantling barriers. Educational institutions often play a pivotal role in shaping perceptions of different faiths. Curricula may lack comprehensive teachings about global religions, creating gaps filled with stereotypes rather than understanding. The failure to engage students in meaningful dialogue leaves them armed with misconceptions as they enter adulthood.

David, an educator in a diverse school district, recognised this shortcoming and spearheaded an initiative to integrate interfaith studies into the curriculum. He reflected,

"I saw firsthand how ignorance breeds fear. Teaching students about the foundational teachings of various religions changed the conversation in our school. Once they understood the core beliefs of Islam and Christianity and how many values overlap, they began to form friendships. That's the power of education—equipping them to challenge stereotypes rather than perpetuate them."

David's approach illustrates the intricate ways in which misunderstandings can be dismantled through awareness and knowledge. Education has the power to cultivate empathy, prompting students to explore shared humanity rather than segregating themselves into siloed ideologies based on misrepresentation.

Additionally, the stories of reconciliation stemming from interfaith dialogues illuminate the potential for growth in personal relationships. Perspectives from individuals who have taken the initiative to engage in challenging conversations reveal an innate human desire for understanding, despite discomfort and vulnerability.

In her journey toward embracing interfaith relationships, Maya, a Christian volunteer at a local mosque, highlights the beauty inherent in such dialogue:

"It can be scary to enter spaces where you feel like an outsider, but that initial discomfort is outweighed by the connections formed through shared experiences. Our conversations challenged me to unpack my assumptions and reassess my beliefs. It opened a door to friendships that are enriching my faith journey."

Maya's story highlights how deepening relationships are born from vulnerability and openness, encouraging readers to consider their roles in fostering environments that promote diverse narratives. The central message resonates throughout the shared experiences: misunderstanding can be transcended through empathy, dialogue, and genuine interaction.

As individuals from both faith backgrounds engage with one another, they discover not only differences but shared values that resonate deeply. The explorations of such exchanges foster opportunities for collaboration that work against the tide of misunderstanding.

To foster these dialogues, community programs that focus on healing and understanding are pivotal. Initiatives that celebrate cultural diversity, similar to Ramadan iftars (daily breaking of fast) or Christmas community service events, can serve to bring individuals together in celebration rather than conflict. These shared experiences can nurture a sense of belonging and belongingness within and between faith communities.

Through celebrating these religious occasions together, Christians and Muslims can cultivate memories that challenge existing prejudices. Spiritual leader, Imam Hassan, emphasises the importance of integration in such celebrations:

"When we gather during Ramadan or Christmas, it's not just us giving, but also receiving. We learn each other's traditions, share stories, and create bonds that transform 'the other' into a friend. We begin to see beyond the labels society has placed upon us."

Christianity and Islam - Two paths, One Purpose

Actively participating in one another's celebrations showcases a commitment to understanding that transcends mere tolerance. It lays the groundwork for a profound exploration of communal identities rooted in respect and shared values.

Yet, there remains the reality that the road to understanding is both challenging and ongoing. As citizens of an increasingly polarised world, it is essential to acknowledge that misunderstandings will not be eliminated overnight. They are often deeply ingrained and fuelled by historical narratives of conflict. Still, each individual has a role to play in either perpetuating or dismantling these narratives.

Christian and Muslim communities must embrace the discomfort of confronting stereotypes, both within their circles and those that surround them. This does not suggest that adhering to one's faith should automatically align with political ideologies or current social agendas; instead, it advocates for individuals to hold space for both personal beliefs and the diversity of experiences they encounter.

In confronting the challenges of misunderstanding, it is crucial to remember that the path forward must incorporate compassion, empathy, and a shared commitment to mutual understanding. By framing conversations through the lens of shared humanity, the narratives that dominate can transform from division into collaboration, paving the way for a future where understanding triumphs over prejudice.

The stories woven throughout this narrative serve as a reminder that clarity can emerge amidst confusion, hope can flicker through darkness, and the power of empathy can reshape the narratives of faith. Although misunderstandings persist, this journey toward reconciliation invites individuals to take on the role of ambassadors of kindness, actively working toward a world that acknowledges differences while cherishing shared values. Each small gesture can create ripples of influence, ultimately fostering a greater sense of unity in our shared humanity.

Contemporary Connections

In a world increasingly defined by division and discord, the call for interfaith understanding grows louder, resonating across diverse communities. The contemporary landscape is coloured with vibrant initiatives that not only acknowledge differences but celebrate similarities, bringing people together through shared values and goals. This subchapter examines various contemporary initiatives aimed at promoting interfaith dialogue and collaboration. By reviewing these initiatives, we uncover the potential for unity, bridging gaps that have long separated followers of different faiths.

A powerful example of interfaith dialogue is showcased in the annual Interfaith Youth Core (IYF) conference, which gathers young people from various backgrounds to engage in discussions about faith, service, and community. Founded by Eboo Patel in 2002, the IYF encourages participants to lead within their communities, using their faith as a source of inspiration for action. The core belief of this initiative is simple yet profound: diverse faiths can work together to create tangible change.

During the IYF conference, young people participate in workshops focused on building skills necessary for interfaith cooperation. Participants, representing Christianity, Islam, Judaism, Hinduism, and more, learn not just to tolerate each other's beliefs but to embrace the richness that diversity brings. Many return to their communities armed with new ideas and relationships, eager to engage others in meaningful conversations about faith and shared humanity. One participant, a young Muslim woman, reflected on her experience, stating, "I understood that my faith is not just a set of beliefs; it is a call to action that resonates deeply with the values of others. I am excited to share what I've learned back home."

In addition to youth engagement, interfaith dialogue has taken root at institutional levels, exemplified by the work of the United Religions Initiative (URI), which was established in 2000 to promote enduring, daily interfaith cooperation. The URI connects grassroots initiatives worldwide, bringing people together to address issues such as poverty, education, and environmental sustainability. Each URI council is comprised of individuals from diverse faith traditions who collaborate on projects that reflect their shared values.

The powerful work done by URI is transformative, as it amplifies the voices of those often unheard. Often, members use storytelling to relay their experiences and inspire others. For example, one council in India combated religious intolerance by organising storytelling events where individuals from different backgrounds recounted personal narratives. This approach not only cultivated empathy but also fostered a sense of common identity amidst diversity. Listening to each other's stories, participants realised that despite different cultural practices, they experienced similar joys and struggles as human beings.

Schools across the globe have also embraced interfaith initiatives, recognising the importance of educating younger generations about religious diversity and empathy. One notable example is the "Faiths Together" program, which introduces students to various spiritual traditions through workshops, discussions, and collaborative community service projects. In one instance, a group of high school students from a Christian school partnered with their Muslim peers to organise a local food drive, demonstrating the power of cooperative action in addressing social issues.

Reflecting on this experience, a student remarked, "It opened my eyes to how much we can achieve when we set aside our preconceptions. Sharing the same goal of helping our community turned into something beautiful—it was about faith in action."

Moreover, initiatives like 'Building Bridges' serve to unite various religious organisations in addressing social justice causes. Rooted in the belief that compassion knows no boundaries, 'Building Bridges' encourages faith leaders to collaborate on action strategies that benefit their communities at large. This campaign not only inspires religious leaders to consider their roles as agents of change but also emphasises the importance of shared moral imperatives in addressing inequality.

In a recent 'Building Bridges' event held in a northern city, leaders from Christian and Muslim communities teamed up to address rising hate crimes. Together, they had a public rally, where they shared messages of solidarity and respect, ensuring community members understood that their faith types did not determine their capacity to stand united against violence or injustice. The event culminated in a statement pledging joint commitment to promote peace, fostering an environment where dialogue flourished.

Social media platforms also act as modern tools for interfaith dialogue, connecting individuals and fostering discussions that transcend geographical boundaries. Initiatives like #InterfaithVoices on Twitter have created a space for individuals to share their experiences, insights, and aspirations related to faith and collaboration. This virtual dialogue enables participants to engage with others from diverse backgrounds, fostering a sense of belonging and promoting empathy.

One popular virtual series titled "Faith in the Digital Age," hosted by various interfaith organisations, showcases faith leaders discussing contemporary social issues through the lens of interreligious understanding. The conversations resonate with viewers as they explore topics such as climate change, racial justice, and mental health from collective perspectives. The series emphasises shared values of compassion and justice that exist across faith traditions, sparking further dialogue among participants and encouraging viewers to seek common ground.

In many communities, interfaith dialogues extend beyond organised events, fostering informal relationships between faith leaders and congregants. These personal connections are vital in combating misunderstandings and prejudices that can lead to hostility. One remarkable effort lies within local organisations that create neighbourhood circles, where diverse community members come together to share meals, celebrate cultural traditions, and learn from one another. These circles afford participants the opportunity to experience differences in a personal, humane manner, ultimately fostering friendship and respect.

As friendships blossom across religious divides, many individuals witness the transformative power of shared humanity. A Christian woman who participated in such a circle described her relationship with a Muslim neighbour, stating, "I never thought I could become so close to someone whose beliefs differ from mine. But through our shared meals and stories, I have learned so much about her faith and my own. We now stand together against misunderstandings in our neighbourhood."

Collaboration in the arts also acts as a powerful medium for interfaith engagement. Through art, communities find common expressions of faith and identity that transcend verbal communication. An initiative called "Art for Unity" has gained traction, bringing together artists from various religious traditions to collaborate on projects that highlight themes of peace, love, and understanding.

For example, a prominent mural unveiled in a diverse urban area depicted representations of different faith traditions, symbolising unity and collective hope for peace. The artists, who hailed from various backgrounds, organised workshops in schools during the mural's inception, engaging students to reflect on the importance of harmony through artistic expression. Through this process, students began to question stereotypes and develop a deeper appreciation for one another, generating meaningful conversations around diversity.

The relevance of everyday humanitarian endeavours in strengthening interfaith relations cannot be overstated. Initiatives focusing on poverty alleviation, climate action, and healthcare unite individuals across religious affiliations while addressing pressing global challenges. Programs such as the "Faiths Against Hunger" campaign pool resources from various faith communities to tackle food insecurity. By collaborating, faith-based organisations have integrated spiritual motivations into actionable plans that demonstrate effective community service.

The recent COVID-19 pandemic underscored the importance of collective action, resulting in numerous interfaith collaborations across communities. In cities worldwide, religious groups partnered to provide essential resources, including food, medical supplies, and emotional support to those in need. Interfaith groups aligned their missions to address vulnerabilities exposed during the pandemic, emphasising compassion and shared responsibility.

A prominent example of this unity during the pandemic occurred when faith leaders organised community vaccination drives, addressing vaccine hesitancy within their communities. By forming alliances, Christian and Muslim leaders engaged in spirited discussions about the ethical implications of vaccination, while also considering their responsibilities toward public health. Ultimately, they came together to advocate for vaccinations as acts of care for others. The effectiveness of their combined efforts not only reflected their commitment to their communities but also set an inspiring precedent for collaborative engagement.

In addition, the narrative of interfaith cooperation is fortified through literature and artistic expression, with many authors utilising storytelling to portray characters from diverse faith backgrounds. Books like "The Faith Club" foster discussions around faith, friendship, and understanding, encouraging readers to reflect on their perspectives about different beliefs. These narratives resonate deeply, imparting lessons about empathy and respect.

One young reader remarked, "Reading about characters from different religions made me think about how interconnected we really are, despite what I might see on the news. It challenged me to be open-minded and seek understanding in my own life."

Educational institutions are increasingly recognising their role in promoting interfaith values, with many universities establishing dedicated interfaith programs. These initiatives often encompass academic courses on interreligious dialogue, workshops, and practical experiences in diverse communities. Such programs empower students to engage with the complexities of religious identity, dismantling stereotypes and fostering multilayered relationships.

For instance, a university in the Midwest established an interfaith leadership program that promotes student cooperation by asking participants to explore how their faith informs their understanding of contemporary societal challenges. As a result, the students collaboratively designed service projects that allowed them to engage authentically with one another. Indeed, this immersive learning experience opened doors to greater appreciation while nurturing subsequent friendships that transcended their differences.

The Digital Age also offers promising tools to promote interfaith understanding beyond traditional approaches. Educational platforms, podcasts, and online courses dedicated to interfaith studies have emerged, empowering believers and seekers alike to explore the framework of dialogue dynamically and engagingly. Virtual forums create safe spaces for healthy discussion while allowing participants to reflect on their respective beliefs openly.

In an age where technology connects people worldwide, social media platforms have proven invaluable for sharing personal stories, insights, and reflections. Initiatives led through platforms like Instagram and Facebook promote interfaith understanding through visual storytelling, starting conversations around shared values. These narratives humanise religious differences, offering direct entry points for connection and collaboration.

Ultimately, the collective engagement of individuals and groups is central to realising a hopeful and transformative vision of interfaith relations. As shared initiatives promote equality, trust, and friendship, followers of various faiths begin to envision a collective future grounded in understanding, respect, and compassionate action. The foundation of unity is built by those who dare to engage, break silos, and embrace a diverse landscape of beliefs.

In the words of one interfaith leader, "When we come together, we don't just build bridges; we build lives filled with hope. Instead of focusing on our differences, we celebrate the common values that bind us together. Our shared world thrives when we invite others in and act with purpose."

As we reflect on these contemporary connections, it's evident that the journey toward interfaith understanding requires continual effort, dedication, and a commitment to fostering relationships. Through the tireless work of individuals and organisations, communities can change narratives that often separate us. The power of shared initiatives underscores the potential inherent in every interaction and collaboration, planting the seeds for empathy to flourish.

This journey reminds us that fostering interfaith understanding is not merely a mission. It is an ongoing commitment to being engaged citizens of the world, actively participating in the dialogue of our time. Through this collective effort, faith is transformed into action, paving the way for a future that values connection over division, unity over hostility, and understanding over judgment.

The Youth's Role

In the intricate tapestry of modern society, the younger generations emerge as powerful threads, weaving a narrative of hope, change, and engagement within their respective faith communities. Their unique perspectives, shaped by a rapidly globalising world, challenge the existing paradigms of faith and spirituality. In this exploration, we delve into how youth movements are not only redefining religious engagement but also advocating for unity, fostering dialogue, and bridging cultural divides.

The world today is marked by unprecedented connectivity, enabling young individuals to communicate, collaborate, and share ideas across borders and cultures. This digital age has fostered an environment in which traditional barriers are less effective, allowing for a cross-pollination of religious and cultural beliefs. It is within this context that the youth of Christianity and Islam find themselves equipped with new tools and platforms to express their faith actively and inclusively.

Transformative Movements: Youth Activism in Faith Communities

One of the most compelling aspects of the youthful engagement with faith is the rise of youth-led movements that challenge the status quo. From grassroots initiatives focused on social justice to larger organisations advocating for interfaith dialogue, these movements are often characterised by passionate individuals who refuse to accept the limitations imposed by tradition.

Take, for instance, the emergence of organisations such as "Muslim Youth for Peace" and "Christian Youth for Justice." These movements have mobilised thousands of young believers to actively engage with pressing social issues such as climate change, poverty, and racial inequity. They seek not only to address these challenges but also to embody the core values of their faiths—compassion, justice, and community service.

The motivations behind these movements often stem from a deep-seated desire for change within their communities. Many young people express disillusionment with established religious institutions, perceiving them as disconnected from the realities of contemporary life. This disconnection, they argue, undermines the relevance of faith in addressing the social injustices and moral dilemmas that pervade their everyday experiences.

One poignant narrative comes from Sarah, a young Muslim activist from Chicago. Having grown up in a community that struggled with violence and poverty, she became committed to serving her neighbourhood through outreach programs that provided mentorship, education, and resources. "Faith should not just be about going to the mosque or church," she says, "It should be about embodying the values of our teachings by lifting each other, especially those who are struggling." Sarah's journey mirrors that of many youths who see their faith as a call to action rather than a set of rituals.

Interfaith Engagement: A New Generation of Bridge Builders

As youth movements gain momentum, interfaith dialogue emerges as a vital means of fostering understanding, respect, and cooperation between Christians and Muslims. Young people today are more likely than previous generations to engage in conversations about faith and spirituality with peers from different religious backgrounds. This openness reflects the interconnectedness fostered by social media and a growing awareness of global issues.

For example, the "Interfaith Youth Core," a prominent organisation founded by Eboo Patel, focuses on generating opportunities for young people to collaborate on community service projects. By working side-by-side, participants—who often come from different faith backgrounds—develop a profound appreciation for one another's beliefs and practices. These collaborative efforts serve not only to address communal needs but also to foster lasting relationships built on mutual respect.

A notable initiative is the "Youth Interfaith Summit," which brings together diverse groups of young leaders from various faiths to discuss pressing social challenges. Through sharing personal stories of faith and hope, attendees develop a collective vision for a more inclusive future. At a recent summit, a young Sikh leader shared her experiences growing up in a predominantly Muslim community, expressing gratitude for the friendships that formed amidst shared struggles.

Another memorable account comes from Amir, a devout Muslim from a suburb of Los Angeles, who participated in a joint Muslim-Christian youth retreat. Through prayer, discussion, and shared meals, Amir realised that while their beliefs might differ in certain respects, the values such as compassion and community service profoundly resonated across faiths. "We may disagree, but we are more alike than we think," he reflected after the retreat, highlighting the transformative power of interfaith engagement.

Challenging Norms: A New Identity in Faith

In their pursuit of more authentic expressions of faith, younger generations are also challenging the norms that have long defined religious practice. This challenge often takes the form of reinterpreting texts, advocating for inclusivity, and seeking justice for marginalised communities within their faith traditions.

In Christianity, movements advocating for LGBTQ+ rights within the church are spearheaded by young believers who envision a faith that embraces all individuals, regardless of sexual orientation. Groups like "The Reformation Project" work tirelessly to foster inclusive communities within traditionally conservative church structures. Young pastors and theologians are increasingly teaching that love and acceptance are at the heart of Christian doctrine, advocating for a theology that affirms LGBTQ+ identities.

Similarly, in Islam, younger generations are actively engaging with concepts such as gender equality and social justice. The emergence of women-led mosques, such as the "Women's Mosque of America," illustrates the desire among young Muslim women to assert their roles as leaders in the faith. By creating spaces for women to pray and engage in religious scholarship, these initiatives challenge patriarchal structures often found within Muslim communities. The voices of women like Aisha, an Imam-in-training in New York, highlight this shift. "We want to create an Islam that is just and equitable," she states. "Engagement in our beliefs means empowering everyone to participate."

The Role of Technology: Digital Faith Engagement

The advent of technology plays a significant role in how young people engage with their faith, transcending physical boundaries and fostering virtual communities. Social media platforms have become powerful tools for spreading messages of unity, inspiration, and activism. From viral hashtags advocating for justice to online prayer circles, digital engagement allows young believers to connect with others globally.

Youth have harnessed these platforms to raise awareness about various issues affecting their communities and beyond. For instance, during the "Black Lives Matter" movement, youth from both faiths used social media to share stories, organise peaceful protests, and encourage collective action. The hashtag #FaithForChange became a rallying cry, uniting members of different backgrounds for a common cause.

In one striking example, a young Christian influencer with a significant following shared videos discussing social justice from a faith perspective, inspiring countless viewers to engage in advocacy work within their religious circles. Meanwhile, a Muslim youth group organised a live-streamed event where participants from different faiths discussed their roles in dismantling systemic injustice. The power of technology becomes even more evident in these instances as both Muslim and Christian youth find common ground in their faith-driven activism.

Finding Common Ground: Joint Initiatives and Collaborations

As youth-led movements continue to gain traction, joint initiatives between Christian and Muslim youth foster a sense of shared purpose and mutual support. One notable example is the "Muslim-Christian Youth Alliance," which has created training programs designed to equip young leaders with skills for advocacy, dialogue, and collaboration.

Through shared workshops and collaborative projects, young people learn about each other's beliefs, engage in skill-building exercises, and morally align on social issues. Participants often express a newfound appreciation for the beauty of their respective faith traditions, leading to meaningful friendships and lasting partnerships.

In larger contexts, events like the "Global Youth Summit," which attracts thousands of young people from various faiths, encourage dialogue on universal themes of dignity, respect, and community responsibility. Attendees participate in workshops that explore the intersection of cultural identity and spirituality, working collaboratively to embrace their diverse heritage while fostering harmonious coexistence.

One participant, a young Christian named David, noted his surprise at discovering the shared values that resonated across faith-based initiatives. "We all want to create a better world. We have different ways of approaching it," he shared, highlighting the realisation that mutual respect and collaboration are key to a unified future.

Reimagining Faith: A Unity Beyond Divisions

In reimagining their faith, young people are not simply adopting new ideologies; they are articulating a vision that emphasises inclusivity, compassion, and a commitment to justice. As they redefine religious engagement, they emphasise the shared values that lie at the heart of Christianity and Islam, promoting a model of faith that transcends doctrinal differences.

This unity is not without its challenges. Resistance from traditionalists within both faith communities can create tensions as young leaders advocate for change. Yet, these challenges often serve to energise youth movements, pushing them to articulate their beliefs with conviction and resilience. The discourse surrounding these movements reflects a broader transformation underway, as they call for faith to be expressed in ways that are relevant and impactful in a modern context.

A collective of young activists recently expressed their commitment to creating change during an interfaith youth conference in Toronto. Standing united, they emphasised the importance of addressing issues such as climate change and social justice from their respective faith perspectives. Their collaborative pledge underscored the understanding that faith can be a unifying force in confronting the world's most pressing challenges.

Mentorship and the Path Forward

As young leaders emerge, mentorship plays a vital role in their development, fostering a culture of shared wisdom and experience. Older generations of faith leaders who are open to dialogue and collaboration can serve as invaluable resources for youth movements, guiding while also respecting the innovative approaches that young people bring.

Programs that promote mentorship between established leaders and youth activists can catalyse meaningful change within faith communities. Such programs encourage both young and old to share experiences, connect over mutual values, and collectively respond to societal issues. A young Christian named Emily, who mentors younger students in her church, shared how this relationship has not only impacted her mentees but has also deepened her understanding of faith and service.

Ultimately, the ongoing interaction between generations will shape the future landscape of faith engagement. Young people are not merely passive recipients of traditions; they are active participants in reimagining how faith can be lived in the 21st century.

Conclusion: The Future of Faith Engagement

As we navigate the complexities of modern faith engagement, the role of youth becomes increasingly significant. Young believers are redefining what it means to live by their faith within a globalised world, crafting narratives that challenge established norms and foster unity. Their movements stimulate interfaith dialogues, promote inclusivity, and advocate for social justice, thereby providing a hopeful vision for the future.

In reflecting on the youth's role within the broader tapestry of Christianity and Islam, we recognise that their passion for change is rooted in the core teachings of compassion and community found in both faith traditions. By engaging with one another and emphasising the shared values that unite them, these young leaders are crafting a new narrative—one that celebrates the diverse expressions of faith while fostering mutual understanding and respect.

As we embrace this narrative, it becomes clear that the path towards unity is not only desirable but essential. In their hands, the future of faith promises to be rich in collaboration, steeped in empathy, and unwavering in its commitment to justice. The language of the youth will continue to shape the discourse around religion and spirituality, affirming that while traditions may differ, the essence of faith can and must bring us together.

Visions for Unity: Pathways to Peace

Fostering Dialogue

In today's increasingly polarised world, fostering dialogue between different faith communities has never been more essential. With diverse perspectives shaping our societies, the potential for misunderstanding and hostility can easily overshadow the shared values that unite us. This subchapter examines the multifaceted approaches to creating spaces for dialogue and understanding, with a focus on techniques that foster cooperation and compassion between Christians and Muslims. By highlighting workshops, conferences, and community gatherings as key methods, we can demonstrate how meaningful exchanges can bridge divides and cultivate friendships across faiths.

The foundation for fostering constructive dialogue begins with the recognition of our shared humanity. Both Christianity and Islam encompass rich traditions that advocate for compassion, respect, and love for one another. Understanding this shared ethos is key to creating a welcoming environment where dialogue can flourish. The journey toward fostering dialogue is a continuous process, one that requires commitment, perseverance, and courage from both faiths.

A significant first step in promoting interfaith dialogue is organising workshops designed to encourage personal connections and shared experiences. These workshops can take various forms, each tailored to address the specific needs and contexts of the participants. One effective model is the "story-sharing workshop," in which participants from both faith communities come together to share personal narratives and experiences related to their faith.

Such workshops can foster an atmosphere of trust and openness, enabling individuals to express their beliefs and feelings while also considering the perspectives of others. By sharing stories of personal struggles, triumphs, and religious practices, participants can uncover the common threads that unite their faiths. For example, a Christian may share how faith guided them through a dark time, while a Muslim can recount a similar experience. The act of storytelling fosters empathy and camaraderie, dismantling preconceptions and opening the door for deeper understanding.

To ground these workshops in meaningful dialogue, facilitators should emphasise active listening skills. Participants should be encouraged to listen not only to respond but to understand. Engaging in reflective listening exercises can further enhance this dynamic, allowing individuals to articulate what they heard and felt while another person spoke. This practice not only affirms the speaker but also deepens the connection between participants by showing that each narrative is valued and respected.

In addition to workshops, interfaith conferences serve as a powerful platform for dialogue. These events can gather scholars, faith leaders, and community members in a larger space to discuss pressing issues affecting both faiths and society. Topics might include social justice, ethical concerns, and shared moral values. By creating panels that represent voices from both Christianity and Islam, attendees gain a broader perspective on the common challenges faced by both communities.

Organising roundtable discussions during these conferences can encourage intimate conversations that invite diverse viewpoints. In contrast to traditional lecture formats, roundtables foster participation and engagement among all attendees. Each participant has the opportunity to voice their thoughts and insights, making it a collaborative forum for exchanging ideas. The format allows for probing questions that can stimulate reflection and encourage critical thinking, thus deepening the dialogue among attendees.

Moreover, these conferences must maintain an inclusive atmosphere that embraces diversity. This can be achieved through various means, including ensuring representation from different cultural backgrounds and demographic groups within both faiths. Addressing intersectional issues, such as race, gender, and socioeconomic status, during discussions opens up avenues for understanding the unique challenges faced by individuals within each faith community.

Equally important are community gatherings, which can serve as a grounding fixture in fostering dialogue at a micro-level. Regularly held gatherings that bring together members of both faiths create opportunities for informal interactions and relationship-building. These events can take the form of potlucks, cultural showcases, or volunteer projects that focus on community service. In bringing people together for a common purpose, participants can develop familiarity and compassion through shared experiences.

One noteworthy example of community gatherings is Interfaith Service Days, where members of both faiths come together to engage in charitable activities. Whether it's a neighbourhood clean-up, food distribution, or support for community shelters, these efforts emphasise the shared commitment to serving humanity. They can break down barriers and build friendships based on mutual goals and shared values, reminding participants that faith is not just about beliefs but also about action.

As community members forge connections through such initiatives, trust and understanding gradually deepen. The informal nature of community gatherings facilitates conversations that might not occur in more structured settings. These spaces allow individuals to ask questions, express curiosity, and explore theological differences without the fear of judgment or confrontation.

Nevertheless, promoting dialogue is not without its challenges. Facilitators must be mindful of the historical tensions and misconceptions that may exist between the two faith communities. Building a safe space for dialogue requires an understanding of these complexities and a commitment to addressing them head-on.

Training and equipping facilitators with the necessary skills to address sensitive topics is essential for the success of these initiatives. Workshop leaders and conference moderators should be prepared to navigate challenging conversations that may arise from personal biases or entrenched beliefs. This aspect of training can help facilitators engage participants empathetically and respectfully, creating opportunities for deeper insights or potential resolutions to misunderstandings.

Additionally, establishing ground rules for dialogue can help attendees articulate their thoughts while maintaining respect for others' perspectives. For instance, establishing rules such as "speak from your own experience" or "avoid interruptions" can create a framework that encourages constructive engagement. By emphasising respect and active listening, participants can navigate discussions, recognising that while opinions may differ, the ultimate goal remains the pursuit of understanding and connection.

Over time, as communities engage in continued dialogue through structured events and informal gatherings, dialogues will evolve.

Relationships built on mutual respect, shared experiences, and meaningful conversations can gradually lay the groundwork for reconciliation and healing. As individuals begin to see their differences as opportunities for growth rather than division, a more profound sense of kinship can emerge.

To amplify the impact of these dialogues, it's crucial to integrate them into educational systems. Schools can serve as vital venues for fostering dialogue between faith communities, where students learn not only about their faith traditions but also those of their peers. Introducing an interfaith curriculum not only encourages empathy and cultural competence but also equips students with the tools to engage in respectful conversations across differences.

One effective educational program is the implementation of interfaith dialogues within youth organisations, such as scout groups, sports clubs, or community service programs. By engaging young people in collaborative activities that emphasise teamwork and communication, participants can develop friendships that transcend religious boundaries while also encouraging them to learn more about each other's faith practices and beliefs. Youth-led initiatives can drive these dialogues forward, empowering the next generation to model patience, understanding, and respect.

For these programs to thrive, it's essential to encourage educators and leaders to participate in training that equips them with skills to facilitate complex discussions. Workshops for educators can provide resources, training, and shared best practices to teach students how to engage others thoughtfully and respectfully about challenging subjects.

Finally, communities should not underestimate the power of online dialogue platforms, especially in an age dominated by technology.

Virtual spaces allow for collective gatherings, where individuals from various geographical locations can engage in discussions conveniently and comfortably. By utilising social media or video conferencing tools, communities can create broader networks of dialogue that extend beyond local boundaries, promoting interfaith talks on a global scale.

Online interfaith forums, webinars, and chat groups can serve as platforms for sharing insights and experiences, bridging geographical divides that may otherwise inhibit grassroots connections. Online spaces can also attract a diverse audience, creating opportunities for cross-cultural conversations that resonate with individuals from different backgrounds.

Nonetheless, while technology offers exciting opportunities for dialogue, it's vital to approach digital interactions with intentionality. In a virtual space, misunderstandings can escalate more easily due to the absence of non-verbal cues, which play a significant role in communication. Promoting healthy online dialogue requires setting norms and guidelines that underscore the importance of respectful interactions.

As we reflect on the importance of fostering dialogue, it becomes clear that the journey toward unity demands intention, creativity, and collective effort. The pathways to peace are paved with intention and exploration, where Christians and Muslims may navigate their differences and discover the shared values that unite them beyond their beliefs.

By creating shared spaces for meaningful dialogue through workshops, conferences, community gatherings, and educational programs, we enable individuals to encounter one another with depth and sincerity. These interactions foster understanding, cultivate meaningful connections, and challenge the narratives that divide us.

Ultimately, the effort to foster dialogue is not just about creating temporary encounters; it is about building long-term relationships that transcend boundaries and foster a sense of belonging. In recognising our shared humanity, we can sow the seeds for a peaceful coexistence rooted in mutual understanding and a commitment to supporting one another's journeys.

The Importance of Education

Education transcends the mere dissemination of information; it shapes the very fabric of society, fostering understanding and empathy among diverse communities. In a world often marked by division, the role of education in promoting interfaith dialogue becomes paramount. This subchapter examines the transformative impact of educational initiatives that incorporate interfaith lessons into the curriculum, drawing on the personal experiences of educators who are pioneering these approaches.

As we explore the significance of education in fostering bridges between Christianity and Islam, it is essential first to understand the impact of curriculum changes that promote mutual respect and understanding. Educational institutions have long served as centres for cultural exchange, yet often they have perpetuated misunderstandings and stereotypes. Recognising this dual role is crucial in crafting a future where students are equipped with academic knowledge and the emotional intelligence and empathy required to navigate a multi-religious society.

One of the foremost educators in this field is Dr. Amina Farah, a seasoned professor of Religious Studies at a community college in a diverse urban area. Dr. Farah has been instrumental in introducing a curriculum that emphasises interfaith dialogue, blending theoretical knowledge with practical engagement. "The goal is to move beyond simply teaching about different religions—to encourage students to experience one another's beliefs intimately and thoughtfully," she shares during an interview.

Dr. Farah incorporates various pedagogical approaches in her courses, including collaborative projects, where students of different faith backgrounds come together to explore their shared values and differences. One such project involves pairing students from Christian and Muslim backgrounds to work on a common goal, such as a community service initiative or a presentation on a theme that resonates across both faiths, like justice or compassion. Here, the classroom transforms into more than just an academic setting; it becomes a microcosm of society, where students can learn firsthand the importance of dialogue, respect, and shared humanity.

The personal accounts of students participating in these projects illustrate the profound impact of education shaped by interfaith dialogue. Amina recounts a transformative experience shared by a student named Sarah, a young Christian woman who initially felt apprehensive about learning alongside her Muslim peers. "She was nervous, thinking she knew little about Islam and feared being judged," Dr. Farah explains. "However, through group discussions and shared community goals, not only did Sarah develop friendships, but she also found herself advocating for the importance of having conversations about faith. She now actively participates in interfaith initiatives beyond the classroom."

These experiences not only nurture a holistic understanding but also cultivate critical thinking skills. As students engage in discussions about challenging topics, such as religious extremism or historical conflicts between their faiths, they learn to analyse and articulate their perspectives respectfully. Dr. Farah emphasises that this engagement is essential: "When students confront these issues head-on, they're better prepared to navigate similar conversations outside the classroom. They develop a vocabulary of respect and understanding that is invaluable in today's polarised society."

The necessity of integrating interfaith dialogue within educational settings extends beyond local classrooms, delving into broader statewide and national policies. Educational leaders worldwide have recognised the benefits of a curriculum that includes interfaith studies. Educational reform has become a focal point for promoting social cohesion in many countries with multi-religious populations.

For instance, in the United Kingdom, the Department for Education has introduced policies that encourage schools to teach about different religions and worldviews in a balanced manner. These efforts seek to dismantle stereotypes and cultivate respect among students. The aim is to educate students about various beliefs and present them as valid choices worthy of understanding. Schools are encouraged to implement projects that foster empathy and critical discussion about faith and culture, prioritising interfaith dialogue in the educational landscape.

One innovative program emerged from a partnership between several secondary schools in London, where educators collaborated to design a unique interfaith curriculum. The "Unity in Diversity" initiative allows students to explore shared values among different faiths through workshops, guest speakers, and interfaith events. One educator involved in the program, Mr. James O'Connor, reflects on the experience: "We wanted our students to not just learn about different religions but to experience the richness these traditions offer. By engaging with peers and community leaders from various faiths, our students have shown significant growth in understanding and acceptance."

Mr. O'Connor introduces a project where students participate in interfaith dialogues and organise community events. "Students become ambassadors of peace in their communities, breaking down the walls of misunderstanding that can lead to conflict," he explains. The narrative of students like Ahmed and Lucy, who first met during a 'Unity Day' event, highlights the power of education in creating connections. Ahmed, a Muslim, and Lucy, a Christian, shared their family traditions during a panel discussion, discovering that they both light candles during major spiritual events, symbolising hope. Their bond illustrates how curricular changes paved the way for genuine friendships anchored in understanding shared human experiences.

Incorporating interfaith dialogue into education cultivates not only understanding but also empathy. Dr. Khadija Malik, an educator from a primary school in Canada, discusses the significance of instilling empathy in young learners. "When children learn about different faiths through stories, art, and collaboration, they learn to see the world through another person's lens," she asserts. Dr. Malik employs a teaching strategy called 'Empathy Circles,' where students share narratives about their religious traditions and personal experiences, encouraging an environment of openness and respect.

"The stories they tell are not just intellectual exercises; they resonate on emotional levels, allowing children to connect and reflect upon their own beliefs. This is where the magic happens," she notes. The compelling narratives shared in these circles lead to in-depth discussions about emotions, identity, and the universality of the human experience. The key takeaway is that empathy is enhanced when students listen to one another and explore the lived experiences of different faith traditions in a structured, supportive environment.

The importance of education in fostering understanding is further underscored by global partnerships aimed at promoting interfaith dialogue. Initiatives like the World Council of Churches and the United Nations Educational, Scientific and Cultural Organisation (UNESCO) have championed educational projects that promote intercultural and interfaith understanding. These projects provide resources and frameworks for schools worldwide to implement curricula that address biases and encourage reconciliation.

A case study from the United Nations highlights an initiative in South Africa, where schools in post-apartheid communities participated in a collaborative interfaith project aimed at addressing lingering divisions. Trained educators facilitated workshops that allowed students from Christian and Muslim backgrounds to engage in joint discussions about their faiths and cultural identities. Evaluations of the program revealed that students reported feeling more comfortable discussing their differences and collaborating to foster positive community relationships.

Educators leading such initiatives often find themselves as mentors and advocates for change, impacting not only their classrooms but also their wider communities. They face challenges in altering traditional curricula that may focus solely on historical conflicts without addressing pathways toward unity and understanding. For many, perseverance becomes essential as they navigate resistance from parents or educational authorities who may question the emphasis on interfaith dialogue.

To foster change on a systemic level, it is critical for educators to collaborate with curriculum committees and policymakers.

Advocacy efforts are necessary to transform curriculum frameworks and state educational standards. Workshops, conferences, and symposiums can serve as valuable platforms for sharing successful pedagogical practices, inspiring educators to integrate interfaith dialogue into their teachings.

For example, a recent symposium on interfaith education held at a prominent university gathered educators, religious leaders, and academics from various backgrounds. The diverse panel discussions highlighted innovative educational strategies that fostered dialogue and cooperation. Participants walked away with practical resources, lesson plans, and networking opportunities to cultivate interfaith learning in their institutions.

The educators who attended the symposium reflected upon their experiences with implementing interfaith dialogue in their classrooms. They noted shifts in student attitudes and increasing interest in social justice issues that connected their learning to real-world challenges. Teachers reported their students beginning to seek out interfaith dialogues voluntarily, initiating conversations outside the classroom that transcended their previous understandings of religious differences.

As educators integrate interfaith studies into their curricula, the importance of supportive communities cannot be overstated. In her role as an Interfaith Education Coordinator, Carol Smith recognises the value of creating networks among educators. "By building a community of practice, we can systematically address challenges and share effective strategies. The collaborative effort allows educators to inspire one another while providing moral support in our shared mission to promote understanding."

With this collaborative spirit, Carol facilitates workshops and training sessions designed to equip educators with the tools and skills necessary to implement effective interfaith dialogue practices. By nurturing supportive professional networks, educators can inspire one another to break down silos and cultivate classroom environments that promote dialogue. In her workshops, Carol emphasises the importance of reflection and adaptation. "Each classroom is unique, and as teachers, we must remain flexible to the needs of our students while still honouring the intention of fostering unity."

As we look toward the future of education and its role in promoting interfaith understanding, it is crucial to remain invested in progressive changes that prioritise dialogue and collaboration. It is imperative to equip the next generation with the skills to thrive in a world that is increasingly interconnected, yet often divided. This requires a conscious effort to create educational spaces that embrace diversity, foster mutual respect, and encourage peaceful coexistence.

In conclusion, the role of education in promoting understanding through interfaith dialogue cannot be understated. The narratives shared by educators like Dr. Amina Farah, Mr. James O'Connor, and Dr. Khadija Malik illustrate the genuine impact of curriculum changes that prioritise empathy, respect, and collaboration. Each personal story reflects a broader movement toward recognising the importance of cultivating understanding among diverse faith communities.

As we envision a future of unity, it is essential to advocate for educational policies that reflect our shared humanity. By investing in interfaith education, we empower students to become advocates for peace—individuals who not only respect their traditions but also honour and appreciate the richness of others. Through education, we can hope to build a world where dialogue fosters a more profound understanding and connection, paving the way for a harmonious future.

Building a Common Future

In an era marked by increasing polarisation and division, envisioning a future where unity supersedes discord is both a challenge and a necessity. The complexities of today's global landscape urge individuals, communities, and nations to seek collaborative pathways. The vision for a harmonious future transcends borders, cultures, and religions; it is a call to recognise our shared humanity above our differences. In this subchapter, we will explore what it means to build a common future, allowing the stories of hope and resilience to guide our aspirations.

To begin, it's essential to reflect on the roots of division and why they persist. History has shown us that misunderstandings often stem from ignorance and fear. In many cases, this fear is fuelled by cultural stereotypes and misrepresented narratives about others. When we isolate ourselves within echo chambers that reinforce preconceived notions, we deny ourselves the opportunity to explore the richness of diverse perspectives. Instead, we should seek to bridge these gaps by fostering dialogue that emphasises empathy and mutual respect.

This endeavour requires intentional actions from individuals and societies. As we embark on this journey toward unity, we must embrace the values of compassion, respect, and open-mindedness. One key aspect of fostering these values is recognising that people are more than just their religious or cultural identities; they are individuals with unique experiences and histories. By celebrating these individual narratives, we empower one another and cultivate a sense of belonging.

Within every community, there exist unheard stories waiting to be shared. It is through these personal narratives that we can find common ground. Let us reflect on the story of two young women—Fatima, a Muslim, and Sarah, a Christian—who lived in a small town where both faiths had coexisted for generations. Initially wary of each other, Fatima and Sarah soon found common interests: their passion for art and their commitment to social justice.

Through their shared love for painting, they began collaborating on an art project that celebrated their diverse cultures while addressing social issues in their community. Their artwork not only bridged the gap between their faiths but also invited others in their town to join in meaningful conversation. As they painted together, they opened their hearts and minds to one another's experiences, resulting in an evolving friendship that challenged their biases and assumptions.

Their powerful story illustrates the transformative potential when individuals from different backgrounds engage in collaborative efforts. It reinforces the idea that genuine connection can erase the boundaries that divide us. Communities around the world can draw inspiration from Fatima and Sarah, utilising creativity and shared interests to overcome stereotypes and build authentic relationships.

Building a common future necessitates a commitment to education, particularly in promoting interfaith understanding. Educational institutions play a crucial role in shaping perspectives from a young age. By incorporating interfaith dialogue into curricula, students gain insights into the beliefs and practices of others, fostering an atmosphere of acceptance and curiosity. Initiatives that bring students from various faith backgrounds together for meaningful conversations can cultivate an environment where respect and understanding flourish.

Consider a collaborative educational program in a multicultural city where schools work together to create interfaith panels, inviting guest speakers from different faith traditions to share their experiences and beliefs. This allows students to see the humanity in others, understanding that despite their differing traditions, they share similar values and aspirations. Education becomes a powerful tool for dismantling prejudice, fostering curiosity, and promoting collaboration.

Conversations about faith don't conclude solely in the classroom. Interfaith initiatives can emerge organically within communities, creating platforms for dialogue and collective action. Community leaders and members from diverse faith traditions can come together to address pressing social issues, including poverty, education, and healthcare. The essence of this collaboration lies in recognising that when we join forces, our impact is significantly magnified, creating ripples of change that benefit all.

For example, in Minneapolis, a unique community project called the Interfaith Action of Greater Saint Paul brings together diverse faith communities to address homelessness. Christian, Muslim, and Jewish congregations collaborate to provide shelter and support to those in need, emphasising their shared commitment to compassion and humanitarian service. By pooling their resources, these communities not only create immediate relief but also foster relationships that transcend barriers, paving the way for deeper understanding and collaboration.

This model of interfaith collaboration can serve as a template for other regions. When faith communities unite through service, the friendships that develop become powerful catalysts for change. Additionally, these interactions can break down preconceived notions about one another, altering the fabric of the community. By championing the importance of unity, these partnerships reflect the strength that diversity can offer.

Art, education, and service act as vital threads that can weave together the fabric of a common future, but we must also address the broader societal structures that fuel division. This requires advocating for policies that promote inclusivity and diversity, urging governments and organisations to embrace multiculturalism as a strength rather than a challenge. Civic engagement, social justice movements, and collaborative governance should prioritise the voices of underrepresented communities, ensuring that policies reflect a commitment to promoting unity across society.

Participants in these movements can embody the spirit of solidarity by becoming advocates for interfaith initiatives. For instance, local leaders from diverse faith backgrounds can join forces to advocate for inclusive policies in their cities, engaging in efforts that reflect the principles of justice and equity. This active engagement sends a powerful message: unity is not merely an ideal; it can be a tangible reality achieved through concerted action.

However, building a common future also means addressing historical grievances that continue to sow discord. Acknowledging past injustices and working towards restorative measures can foster healing and reconciliation. Faith leaders and community activists can facilitate spaces for dialogue where individuals share their experiences and confront historical wounds. Acknowledgement is often the first step toward healing, and the recognition of shared suffering can create new avenues for understanding.

Take, for example, the story of two communities that experienced conflict due to religious differences. Leaders from both sides engaged in a peacebuilding initiative focused on truth-telling and restorative justice. By creating safe spaces for dialogue, they allowed community members to share their pain and acknowledge historical injustices. The process not only fostered healing but also inspired a collective commitment to collaborate in building a more inclusive future. Their efforts exemplify how confronting historical divides can pave the way for transformative healing.

Ultimately, the creation of a common future is not an endpoint but a continual journey—a commitment to uphold the values of collaboration, understanding, and inclusivity. It requires ongoing effort and a willingness to engage in often uncomfortable conversations that challenge our perceptions. Each small step towards unity contributes to the larger narrative of our shared humanity.

As we contemplate our roles in this shared journey, it is vital to engage in self-reflection. We must ask ourselves: how can we contribute to a future where collaboration and compassion take precedence over division? The answers may vary, but they often involve taking actions both big and small, grounded in our capacity for empathy and honesty.

We must consider engaging with individuals from diverse backgrounds, listening to their stories, and sharing our journeys. Wherever we find ourselves—be it in our families, workplaces, or places of worship—there are opportunities to build bridges. Encouraging respectful dialogue, fostering relationships, and becoming allies in moments of injustice can transform the narrative we collectively create.

Personal accountability also plays a role in shaping the collective response to challenges. Each of us can choose to be advocates for unity in our circles, promoting inclusivity and dispelling myths about others. By sharing stories of collaboration and understanding, we can inspire others to join us on the path to unity.

In closing, envisioning a future where unity supersedes division is not merely aspirational; it is essential. Just as threads woven together create a tapestry, our collective efforts can build a rich and meaningful future. We learn from the narratives of individuals who challenge us to think differently and embrace diversity. Every story shared contributes to a larger narrative that reflects our interconnectedness.

As we embark on this journey, let us celebrate the beauty of diversity while actively working toward unity. Whether through art, education, service, engagement, or dialogue, we possess the capacity to foster a common future. The call to action is clear: let us commit ourselves to building a world where mutual respect and understanding thrive, illuminating our path toward peace and collaboration. Together, we can rise to the occasion, laying the groundwork for a future not divided by faith or culture but strengthened by our shared humanity.

Voices of the Faithful

Personal Journeys

In a world marked by division and misunderstanding, the personal stories of individuals can illuminate the shared human experience. Personal journeys of faith, often filled with challenges and breakthroughs, reveal the transformative power of belief, grounding abstract concepts in the tangible experiences of real people. This subchapter aims to highlight diverse stories from followers of Christianity and Islam, reflecting on how faith shapes identities, community interactions, and personal resilience. Each narrative serves to bridge the gap between faith traditions, fostering empathy and understanding between readers and their journeys.

Emily's Walk of Faith

Like many young women navigating the complexities of contemporary life, Emily found herself at a crossroads in her beliefs. Raised in a devout Christian family in a small town in the Midwest, Emily was immersed in the rich traditions of her faith from an early age. Her childhood was filled with Sunday school teachings, summer church camps, and community outreach projects. Yet, as she transitioned into adulthood and moved to a bustling city for college, the security of her childhood faith began to wane.

In the vibrant tapestry of university life, Emily encountered a spectrum of beliefs and lifestyles that challenged her own. It was in this diverse environment that she met Layla, a Muslim student who soon became one of her closest friends. Over cups of coffee and late-night study sessions, Emily and Layla shared not only their academic pursuits but also their spiritual journeys. Despite their differing faiths, the two young women discovered their shared struggles—questions of identity, purpose, and belonging.

Emily began to explore her faith more deeply, questioning the tenets she had taken for granted. She attended Bible study groups at her university, engaging in discussions that invited differing interpretations and perspectives. It was during these discussions that she first encountered the concept of doubt as an essential part of faith—an idea she had never fully embraced before. Despite feeling unmoored at times, this new understanding liberated her. It allowed her to explore the depths of her spirituality without the fear of rejection.

In conversations with Layla, she discovered parallels in their faith narratives. Layla spoke about her experiences growing up in a Muslim household, the beauty of Ramadan, and her commitment to community service through Zakat. Both women's faiths emphasised compassion, community, and the importance of serving others. Inspired by Layla's commitment, Emily sought to translate her own beliefs into action. Together, they volunteered for a local homeless shelter, where they shared stories, laughter, and even tears with people from various walks of life.

Emily's journey was not without conflict. Throughout college, she faced criticism from some peers who felt her friendship with Layla compromised her Christian values. Yet, rather than walking away from her faith, Emily embraced the challenge. She began to see her friendship as a testament to the core tenet of Christianity: to love one's neighbour. This perspective was solidified during a challenging summer when she broke her leg, a situation that prompted her church community to rally around and support her in extraordinary ways.

Christianity and Islam - Two paths, One Purpose

That summer, as she recovered, Emily reflected on the power of support, understanding, and love—values that are echoed in both Christianity and Islam. Her journey culminated during her final year of college, when she organised an interfaith panel at her university, inviting speakers from Christian and Muslim backgrounds to share their narratives. This event not only fostered dialogue among students but also deepened her faith, reinforcing her identity as a compassionate individual who could navigate the rich, complicated tapestry of human beliefs.

Ali's Path to Acceptance

Ali, a young man from a middle-class family in a suburb of London, grew up surrounded by the rich traditions of Islam. His parents, immigrants from Pakistan, instilled in him a strong sense of cultural heritage and religious duty. Yet, as he entered his teenage years, Ali began to feel the weight of expectation that often accompanied his faith. He struggled with the traditional views of masculinity and faith he encountered at home, feeling an intense pressure to conform to established norms that he found increasingly stifling.

In his search for acceptance, Ali explored various aspects of his identity, finding solace in writing. He penned poems that captured the contradiction of his life—his desire to honour his heritage while forging a path that felt authentic to him. His writing expressed his frustration with external expectations and his aspiration to carve out his own identity. His discovery of spoken word poetry provided an outlet for him to voice his experience, gaining recognition at local open mic nights. Poetry became a bridge for Ali, allowing him to connect with others despite cultural differences.

Throughout this period, Ali met Sarah, a devout Christian who shared his passion for art and community service. With Sarah, he felt comfortable discussing faith without judgment. She encouraged him to embrace both sides of his heritage and helped him see that it was okay to question traditions that felt limiting. He found himself captivated by the similarities in their beliefs—the emphasis on charity, community support, and a call to live generously.

As his friendship with Sarah deepened, so did Ali's understanding of faith. He began attending her church services, fascinated by the warm communities he observed. During conversations with Sarah, he discovered stories from the Bible that mirrored experiences from his own life and those found in the Qur'an. This realisation ignited a passion for learning, prompting Ali to explore interfaith dialogues and outreach programs that fostered understanding between different religions.

However, Ali's journey was significantly challenged when he faced backlash from within his community. After expressing his desire to explore Christianity and his growing friendships with Christian peers, he encountered resistance from family members and friends who held firmly to their beliefs about preserving cultural identity. Their concerns weighed heavily on him, and he faced a profound sense of loneliness.

Navigating this tumultuous landscape, Ali turned back to writing. He poured his feelings into his work, crafting pieces that articulated the struggle between tradition and personal truth. His poetry became a channel for healing, helping him articulate the complexities of his journey. Eventually, he shared some of these pieces at interfaith gatherings, where he received overwhelming support and appreciation for his vulnerability.

Ali's experience culminated when he found a balance between honouring his family traditions and embracing a broader understanding of faith. Through open dialogues and the courage to assert his identity, he fostered deeper connections with those around him, including his family, who began to respect his perspective. His journey serves as a testament to the transformative power of self-awareness and the beauty of faith as a guiding force toward unity.

Aisha's Journey of Discovery

Aisha grew up under the bright sun of Morocco, surrounded by the vibrant colours of her culture and the rich traditions of her Islamic faith. Born into a family deeply rooted in spirituality, Aisha's childhood was steeped in the values of compassion, gratitude, and respect. She grew up learning about Islam from her grandmother, whose tales of the Prophets and their trials captivated her imagination.

As Aisha transitioned into adolescence, she found herself grappling with the expectations placed upon her as a young Muslim woman in a rapidly changing world. Like many young people, Aisha yearned for independence and sought to carve out her own path. She was fascinated by Western culture, often questioning how her faith would fit into the global narrative of progressive identity.

While studying at a university in a cosmopolitan city, Aisha encountered an array of ideas that both excited and frightened her. Among her friends, she met Jasmine, a Christian woman who was also navigating her journey of self-discovery. Despite representing different faiths, Aisha and Jasmine struck a chord with each other, realising they shared everyday struggles related to belonging and the desire for acceptance.

Through their conversations, Aisha began to recognise the richness within both of their traditions, discovering how concepts of justice, mercy, and love transcended cultural boundaries. There was an undeniable beauty in the way they celebrated their respective faiths, revealing that their journeys were less about differences and more about shared values.

However, Aisha faced moments of intense internal conflict as she balanced her newfound friendships with her traditional upbringing. Notifications from her family and community regarding her associations and choice of clothing often seeped into her mind, causing her to question her identity. During this tumultuous period, she took a trip to Mecca for pilgrimage, a journey meant to reconnect her with her faith.

Standing amidst the crowds of pilgrims, Aisha felt a sense of belonging that transcended individual identities. The experience solidified her understanding of Islam as a faith that embraces diversity and encourages seeking knowledge. Inspired by this realisation, Aisha returned home with renewed vigour, determined to pursue her passions while honouring her faith.

With Jasmine's encouragement, Aisha founded a student organisation aimed at fostering interfaith understanding within campus life. They organised workshops and discussion panels that encouraged students to share their stories and engage with one another. Aisha's journey transformed into one of leadership, amplifying minority voices and promoting unity, teaching the importance of empathy and respect through tangible actions.

Ultimately, Aisha's story is one of empowerment and self-discovery, illustrating that living one's faith is not a destination but a lifelong journey, full of explorations, questions, friendships, and transformative experiences.

Christianity and Islam - Two paths, One Purpose

David's Reconciliation with Tradition

David, a Jewish convert to Christianity, provides yet another layer of personal journey within the shared landscapes of faith. Growing up in a secular household in London, David's exploration of spirituality began in his late teens when he felt a yearning for something deeper. After a profound experience at a community service project, David sought out a faith that would embrace both his desire to serve and his quest for meaning.

Initially drawn to Judaism, he immersed himself in Hebrew scriptures and traditional practices, exploring the richness of customs and history. However, as David delved deeper, he discovered elements of Christianity that resonated with him profoundly—the themes of love, forgiveness, and redemption echoed in the teachings of Jesus. He felt a strong pull towards the New Testament, revealing to him a narrative of grace that transcended ritual.

After years of contemplation, which included studying alongside rabbinical scholars and Christian pastors, David decided to convert to Christianity. Yet, the moment he announced his choice to his Jewish family was fraught with tension. Many in his community felt betrayed, and their reactions ranged from disappointment to outright hostility. The rift tore at David's heart, challenging his convictions and commitment to love, which he believed was central to both his faith and that of his wife.

As he navigated this conflict, David found solace in the inclusive teachings of Christianity. Through outreach initiatives aimed at addressing societal issues, David used his unique perspective to bridge understanding between faith communities. One of his significant achievements was organising a citywide interfaith event that brought together Jewish, Muslim, and Christian leaders to discuss social justice issues facing their communities.

David's story illustrates the complexities of conversion and the often-painful process of seeking acceptance. He faced the struggle of reconciling the values he cherished with the expectations of others, ultimately discovering that his faith could serve as a means of unification rather than division.

Through immense personal growth, David embraced both his past and present, focusing on building bridges rather than highlighting differences. His journey exemplifies the learnings that arise when one opens their heart to explore faith beyond preconceived boundaries—a testament to the human spirit's ability to seek unity through love and understanding.

Sofia's Two Worlds

Sofia, a first-generation Cameroonian descendant, grew up in a household that straddled two cultures. Her father, a practising Catholic, instilled traditional values of faith, while her mother, a lifelong Muslim, embraced the teachings of Islam. As a child, Sofia revelled in the vibrant celebrations that filled her home, from Christmas festivities to Eid family gatherings. However, as she grew older, the duality of her identity began to weigh heavily on her.

In high school, Sofia became acutely aware of her cultural complexity in her peer group. Friends often posed questions—sometimes innocently, sometimes accusatorily—about her faith. As classmates debated the differences between Christianity and Islam, Sofia felt caught in an uncomfortable terrain, unprepared to articulate her own identities amidst the noise of misunderstanding.

Christianity and Islam - Two paths, One Purpose

Determined to embrace her multicultural heritage, Sofia found strength in the principle of respect that both faiths underscored. It fuelled her passion for interfaith dialogue, pushing her to organise events that encouraged conversations about shared values. She collaborated with local religious leaders to create community forums where individuals could voice their experiences and learn from one another.

Through these initiatives, Sofia discovered that sharing food—a universal symbol of hospitality—broke down barriers. Culinary events evolved into cultural exchanges, where friends from diverse backgrounds gathered together to share meals, bonding over stories and laughter.

Sofia often reflected on how her family's commitment to both faiths allowed her to cultivate a unique sense of belonging. Instead of viewing her dual identity as a conflict, she perceived it as a blessing that enriched her understanding of community, love, and service. Her journey towards self-acceptance illuminated the path for others in her community to embrace their own multifaceted identities.

Sofia's journey ultimately highlights the resilience of the human spirit in the face of complexity, revealing how faith can provide strength, foster understanding, and bridge cultural divides.

Conclusion

The stories of Emily, Ali, Aisha, David, and Sofia exemplify the intricate landscape of faith, illustrating how personal journeys are often fraught with tension but ultimately lead to profound understanding and growth. Each narrative resonates with universal themes of discovery, acceptance, and the power of community, serving as a testament to the beauty of embracing diversity in a world marked by division.

These journeys remind us that faith is not a monolithic experience but a complex and evolving journey that shapes our identities. By sharing these heartfelt stories, we enrich the dialogue surrounding faith and inspire readers to view the tapestry of beliefs with compassion and understanding, fostering a collective journey toward unity.

Common Struggles

The world we inhabit is filled with complexities that can often lead believers from both Christianity and Islam to confront similar struggles throughout their spiritual journeys. These common challenges weave a narrative of shared experiences that transcend doctrinal differences, enriching not only one's faith but also the broader relationships between the two communities. Recognising and addressing these shared struggles fosters a greater sense of empathy and understanding, nurturing bonds that can unite followers of both faiths.

Doubt is a fundamental aspect of faith that can manifest in various forms. For both Christians and Muslims, periods of uncertainty often surface, leading to profound questions about their beliefs, the nature of God, and the implications of their faith in daily life. While it may be tempting to view doubt as a weakness, it can also be a catalyst for growth. For many believers, doubt prompts exploration, dialogue, and a deeper understanding of their sacred texts. The journey through doubt can be isolating, yet it is a universal aspect of the human experience.

Think about Sarah, a Christian who has spent years devoted to her church community. Raised in a household that revered the tenets of the Bible, she always adhered to the teachings of her faith. However, following a personal tragedy—the loss of her mother to an unexpected illness—she found herself grappling with inconsolable grief. The foundational beliefs she had held since childhood began to tremble under the weight of her sorrow. "How can a loving God allow such pain?" she often questioned. These thoughts led to sleepless nights and an overwhelming sense of isolation. In her despair, she stumbled upon a support group for grieving individuals, where she met Ahmed, a practising Muslim affected by his tragedy.

Ahmed, too, had lost a loved one—a close friend and fellow community member—who died in a tragic accident. Just like Sarah, he felt abandoned by his faith amid his grief. "I prayed for fairness, for answers, for any sign that God was still with me," he shared in a moment of vulnerability. The discussion that unfolded between him and Sarah was not merely one of grief but an exploration of how each had processed their angst and searched for hope simultaneously.

Through shared experiences, both found a sense of camaraderie that transcended their religious identities. They expressed their doubts without fear of judgment, learning that in this sacred space, their vulnerability did not detract from their faith; instead, it enhanced it. Their exchanges led to mutual support, illuminating the similarities in their journeys, while also laying the groundwork for interfaith understanding. Their conversations revealed that in times of doubt, both faiths encourage believers to seek solace not only in scripture but also within their communities.

Resilience is another theme that echoes through the struggles faced by both Muslims and Christians. Life's trials can be overwhelming, yet many followers channel their faith into creating stories of hope and strength. Within Christianity, the concept of perseverance is often illustrated through the biblical figure of Job, whose unwavering faith in the face of catastrophic loss serves as a paragon of resilience. Job's torment inspired countless believers to find strength in despair, compelling them to hold on to hope when faced with adversity. Similarly, the story of the Prophet Muhammad's life is a testament to resilience, as he faced persecution that tested his faith and commitment to his mission. His determination to maintain a message of compassion and mercy in the face of hostility resonates deeply with Muslim believers, providing a focal point for strength and perseverance in their trials.

Consider Daniel, a young pastor, who faced dire circumstances when a devastating flood struck his community, displacing countless families and damaging homes. Instead of succumbing to despair, Daniel organised relief efforts, calling upon his congregation to uplift those in need. Working side by side with local organisations, including a nearby mosque, his initiative fostered healing within the community. Believers of different faiths came together to provide food, shelter, and emotional support, forming unlikely alliances that demonstrated the power of resilience in the face of tragedy.

Likewise, Aisha, a Muslim woman, found herself navigating cultural challenges as an immigrant. When she first arrived in a new country, she struggled to find her place, battling feelings of isolation and a sense of not belonging. Yet, in the face of adversity, she chose to empower herself by joining community outreach programs that educate marginalised groups about cultural diversity. Her resilience manifested not only in her journey but in the lives she touched. Aisha's story resonated with Daniel's, for both individuals exhibited how faith can embolden one to serve and uplift others during challenging times.

Christianity and Islam - Two paths, One Purpose

In both labyrinths of doubt and resilience, shared experiences echo deeply human themes: the quest for hope amid uncertainty and the urge to seek meaning through life's challenges. These narratives often compel believers to confront deep-seated questions about existence, faith, and their interconnectedness. Through shared struggles, Christians and Muslims can understand that their lives are interwoven, sparking bridges of empathy that are essential in a world often divided.

Hope, perhaps, is the most unifying theme of all. In an age replete with upheaval, both faith communities face similar societal pressures, which can give rise to scepticism about relationships between their traditions and broader realities. Yet, amidst these pressures, believers continue to find glimmers of hope that inspire perseverance in their faith journeys. Stories of hope can serve as reminders that even in moments of despair, light can emerge through the darkness.

Take the story of Miriam and Fatima, two friends from different faith backgrounds who found solace and support in each other. Both faced challenges as they navigated their roles as mothers during times of social unrest. Miriam often felt overwhelmed by the pressures of raising her children in an environment rife with misunderstanding and division. At the same time, Fatima encountered similar concerns about preserving her daughters' faith and identity in a society that seemed to strip them away. Together, the two women embarked on a journey of collective support, forging a bond that unearthed a shared vision for their families.

Miriam soon recognised that Fatima's perspectives broadened her understanding of the intricacies of theological teachings that resonated across their faiths. Meanwhile, Fatima began to appreciate the significance of community parenting with Miriam. Their conversations blossomed into collaborative efforts, including joint family events that celebrated cultural differences while emphasising shared values like compassion and loving-kindness. Their activism and education illuminated paths of hope that inspired not only their family units but also the wider community.

Through the lens of their struggles, both women contribute to a collective story where faith merges with activism and a commitment to nurturing future generations. The optimism fostered by shared vulnerabilities exemplifies how faith can guide individuals to positively impact the world, creating bonds that mend the fabric of their communities.

The struggles that Christians and Muslims face often serve as catalysts for conversations that enhance understanding between communities. Each story shared reinforces the notion that both traditions ultimately seek hope, wholeness, and connection. The individuals who traverse these paths are essential not only for building bridges of understanding but also for creating dialogue spaces rooted in compassion and respect. When believers from either faith encounter shared struggles, they become agents of change, moving towards systemic understanding that can dissolve prejudice and foster unity.

In conclusion, the shared struggles faced by followers of Christianity and Islam—doubt, resilience, and hope—forge deep connections between individuals despite apparent differences. The stories of Sarah and Ahmed, Daniel and Aisha, and Miriam and Fatima illuminate the threads that unite them, laying a foundation for empathy and compassion. By highlighting these commonalities, we open ourselves to a world where interfaith dialogue flourishes, paving the way for a harmonious existence. Acknowledging these common challenges not only nurtures personal growth in believers but also creates a ripple effect that extends beyond the confines of their respective faiths, paving the way for a shared journey of understanding that celebrates their shared humanity. This path forward invites all of us to participate in the collective pursuit of peace and connection, enriching the shared tapestry of the human spirit.

Stories of Reconciliation

In a world often divided by belief systems, biases, and centuries-old conflicts, the stories of reconciliation between individuals from different faiths reveal a powerful truth: common humanity can overshadow differences, and friendship can blossom in the most unexpected situations. The narratives that follow showcase moments of understanding, dialogue, and connection, emphasising the transformative power these interactions hold not just for individuals but also for communities.

In a small town nestled in the heart of the United States, a Christian woman named Sarah found herself perplexed by the growing tensions between her community and the local Muslim population. After a particularly virulent backlash against a nearby mosque, which was the target of hate speech and vandalism, Sarah felt compelled to act. Rather than joining her neighbours in their protests, she chose instead to reach out.

Sarah began attending interfaith dialogue events organised by a community centre that aimed to bridge the gap between religions. It was there that she met Amina, a bright and articulate Muslim woman who had recently moved to the town with her family. Amina shared her experiences of Islamophobia, expressing how the attacks on the mosque deeply affected not only her community's faith but also their daily lives.

Over cups of tea in a quiet corner of the centre, the two women began to build a rapport. Despite their differing beliefs, they discovered a mutual love for community service and a desire to promote understanding among their peers. Sarah and Amina soon collaborated on a local initiative called "Neighbours Together" that aimed to foster connection through shared community projects, such as food drives and clean-up efforts. The project's unveiling attracted attention and sparked curiosity, inviting people from both communities to come together.

As the months passed, participants of "Neighbours Together" began to share personal stories and experiences, leading to discussions that transcended their initial biases. Many discovered shared values—love for family, dedication to service, and a commitment to peace—that helped to dismantle animosities. Through the success of their joint efforts, Sarah and Amina became not only friends but also advocates for understanding and respect in their community, proving that reconciliation is not only possible but essential.

Similarly, the narrative of reconciliation found its way into the life of Amir, a Muslim teenager in a city marked by division. In school, he faced daily ridicule from classmates who held prejudiced views shaped by negative stereotypes. Amid this hostile environment, Amir found solace in the art room, where he channelled his frustration into painting.

One afternoon, while showcasing his latest artwork at a local exhibit, Amir drew the attention of Emily, a Catholic girl whose family had raised her to abstain from judgment. Intrigued by Amir's work, Emily approached him to ask about the meaning behind his paintings. What started as a simple conversation blossomed into a deeper exploration of each other's stories.

Emily's genuine curiosity prompted Amir to share his experiences in navigating life as a Muslim youth in a predominantly non-Muslim neighbourhood. Through their conversations, Emily learned not only about Amir's cultural background but also about the shared struggles that youth face, regardless of faith—bullying, self-identity, and the search for belonging.

As their friendship grew, Emily invited Amir to participate in a school project advocating against bullying. Together, they created an awareness campaign that allowed students to voice the pain of exclusion and advocate for kindness and acceptance. Their project became more than an assignment; it sparked critical discussions around diversity and respect within their school community.

Another compelling story of transformation comes from the experience of two families, one Muslim and one Christian, brought together through a food network initiative in an urban neighbourhood. The Ali family had settled in the community a few years prior and became known for their delicious homemade samosas. Similarly, the Rivera family was known for their traditional tamales and had long been part of the fabric of the neighbourhood.

When a local non-profit launched a program encouraging neighbours to share cultural recipes and learn from one another, the Ali and Rivera families found themselves working side by side in the kitchen. Initial hesitations were quickly replaced with laughter and storytelling over pots simmering with spices.

As they shared recipes, they also exchanged traditions, personal anecdotes, and reflections on faith. They discovered that their religious practices, while different in ritual, shared an essence of compassion and generosity towards others. Gatherings of neighbours around shared meals became the ultimate symbol of acceptance, empowering both families to host larger community dinners that invited others from various backgrounds to join.

As the bonds deepened, the Ali and Rivera families recognised that the act of sharing food was about more than just culinary exchange—it represented a reconciliation of cultures and healing of misconceptions. Through their efforts, entire neighbourhoods began to shift perspectives, as guests were far more likely to return the invitation and engage in the myriad voices that coloured their community.

The International Institute for Peacebuilding hosted a workshop where a group of Christian and Muslim participants from conflict-affected regions shared harrowing stories related to violence and loss. Among them were Maya, a Christian woman who had lost family members to sectarian violence, and Nasir, a Muslim man who had experienced forced displacement due to the same conflict.

Initially, the two sat at opposite ends of the room, their hearts heavy with hurt and anger. However, as the workshop facilitators encouraged storytelling, Maya and Nasir found themselves gradually sharing their experiences. The dialogue allowed them to articulate not only the pain inflicted upon their communities but also their hopes for reconciliation.

Maya openly wept as she recounted her loss, and Nasir recounted tales of friendship with Christians when he was a child. It became a poignant moment for both, as they understood that their experiences were intertwined. This realisation became the turning point of their budding friendship.

Christianity and Islam - Two paths, One Purpose

Through repeated dialogues, Maya and Nasir promulgated the idea that reconciliation transcends grievances and allows healing to flourish. They went on to establish a community-led initiative focusing on peace education in schools, teaching children from both faiths to embrace their shared humanity over hatred.

As a seasoned pastor and a figure of authority in his own congregation, he reflected on interfaith dialogue and expressed a sincere wish for more clergy and lay leaders to participate. During his journey, he attended a local interfaith gathering, where he met Imam Malik, a Muslim leader. Rather than viewing each other through the lens of their religious titles, they engaged in discussions about societal challenges affecting both their communities.

In a compelling exchange, the pastor shared his struggles with congregants who feared interactions with Muslims due to their prejudices. Imam Malik listened intently, nodding in understanding, until he finally responded with his challenges regarding perceptions of Islam.

Their conversations became a powerful narrative of trust and broken barriers. The duo decided to work together, creating public events that invited dialogues alongside shared meals, ultimately mobilising their communities to challenge the status quo of hatred. They invigorated a sense of kinship that had once seemed improbable, breaking down stereotypes one conversation at a time.

Reconciling friendships were also formed on college campuses. Samira, a Muslim student, and Jake, a Christian student, were assigned to work together on a project examining socio-political issues faced by both Christianity and Islam in contemporary contexts. Initially apprehensive, the two began their collaboration with a trepidation borne of external stereotypes.

However, as they delved into their research, they came to recognise the similarities in their backgrounds and experiences, particularly concerning issues of discrimination and marginalisation in society. Through long hours spent discussing their project, they exchanged cultural insights and spiritual narratives, allowing the veil of prejudice to fall away.

Their project culminated in a presentation at an interfaith symposium, where they drew connections between the political dilemmas faced by both faiths and the societal responsibility of young leaders in fostering understanding. Samira and Jake quickly became recognised not only for their academic prowess but also for their unyielding friendship that became an exemplar of interfaith cooperation on campus.

The beauty of these stories lies in their authenticity and the rawness of overcoming prejudice through personal connection. One of the most profound realisations is the understanding that peace is not merely the absence of conflict but the presence of a relationship grounded in respect and mutual appreciation. Each narrative serves as a testament to the transformative power that comes from intentional dialogues, enabling individuals to embrace the dignity of one another's experiences.

As the world grapples with sectarian divisions fuelled by misunderstanding and fear, it is imperative to share these stories of hope far and wide. Each tale of reconciliation echoes a universal truth: friendship can triumph over scepticism, collective action can overcome prejudice, and through understanding, the seeds of mutual respect can flourish, reminding us of the shared threads that bind all of humanity.

Christianity and Islam - Two paths, One Purpose

In the quiet corners of cities, amid the fervour of university campuses, and the halls of community centres, people are working tirelessly to champion understanding. Whether forging friendships over meals, collaborating on service projects, or simply listening to the stories of those whose lives differ from our own, these individuals are a testament to the idea that relationships built on empathy can heal the deepest divides.

Like vibrant threads woven into the intricate tapestry of life, these narratives urge readers to take actionable steps in their communities. Whether it is starting conversations, promoting interfaith engagement, or standing against injustice, these stories assert the power inherent within each human interaction. Faith must not be a barrier but a bridge, proving that understanding and fellowship can emerge from the shared human experience.

As Sarah and Amina, Amir and Emily, the Ali and Rivera families, Maya and Nasir, and countless other voices exemplify, the stories of reconciliation illuminate a path forward. A path that not only honours complexity but also serves as an invitation for all to participate in the evolving narrative of peace, dialogue, and acceptance in a world where too often differences eclipse our shared humanity.

In Closing: One Humanity, Many Threads

Reflections on Our Shared Journey

As we conclude our exploration of the intertwining journeys of Christianity and Islam, we find ourselves in a moment ripe for reflection—an opportunity to appreciate the shared history of these two great faiths that have shaped millions of lives across centuries and continents. In the grand tapestry of human civilisation, these religions, while distinct in their teachings and practices, intermingle in profound ways that speak to shared values, everyday struggles, and aspirations for a better world.

To begin, let us acknowledge the foundational threads that weave Christianity and Islam together. Both faiths trace their origins back to the same geographical and historical context, where the ancient narratives of humanity were birthed. From the cradle of civilisation in Mesopotamia, the stories of patriarchs like Abraham forge a bond that has influenced not only their respective religious paradigms but has also guided ethical and moral standards throughout the ages. Abraham stands as a symbol of monotheism—a shared belief in one God—whose legacy reverberates within the rites and doctrines of both faiths. Reflecting on this shared ancestry, it becomes evident that, despite theological divergences, a profound respect for the divine has been a common touchstone for both communities.

In the chapters preceding this one, we examined the role of historical figures such as Jesus and Muhammad and how their teachings offer insights into the human condition. While their messages differ

Christianity and Islam - Two paths, One Purpose

significantly—Jesus conveying the new covenant of grace and love, and Muhammad emphasising the oneness of God and the importance of submission—both figures have inspired legions of followers. They cast light on humanity's yearning for purpose, love, and community, illustrating the innate desire to find meaningful connections with God and one another. This reflection on their lives prompts us to think about how we can draw upon their legacies in our modern world, where division often overshadows unity.

The shared narratives explored throughout this book highlight many familiar figures and stories, from Adam to Mary, whose lives manifest virtues such as perseverance, compassion, and faith. By acknowledging these overlapping narratives, we open ourselves to a deeper understanding of the heart of both traditions. This exploration beckons us to move beyond mere theological discourse; it urges us to embrace a shared humanity that transcends differences.

As we zoom out from individual narratives to the broader historical context, we observe that interactions between Christians and Muslims have varied significantly throughout the ages, marked by both collaboration and conflict. The Golden Age of Islam, characterised by a flourishing of knowledge, philosophy, and the arts, vividly illustrates a time when scholars across the faiths could work together, advancing human understanding. Figures such as Averroes and Al-Farabi contributed to a foundation of philosophical thought that would later influence the Renaissance in Europe, embodying an era where faith and reason walked hand in hand.

However, history also contains shadows—points of conflict that bred sectarian tension, most notably during the Crusades. These periods of hostility serve as reminders of what is at stake when misunderstanding and mistrust prevail. Yet even amidst division, moments of reconciliation emerged. Stories from the Crusades often reveal how interfaith dialogue sparked unexpected friendships. When faced with a common enemy, many found solace in shared humanity, leading to alliances that crossed the boundaries of faith.

In our modern context, we stand on the shoulders of this history, challenged to address the misconceptions and stereotypes that perpetuate division. Misunderstandings can cloud the perceptions of both Christians and Muslims, with each community often shaped by external narratives that do not accurately reflect the essence of the other. As we navigate these complexities, it is essential to foster an environment that encourages truthful dialogue to flourish. This calls for courageous conversations, where individuals from both faiths can share their stories, dispel myths, and extend a hand of friendship.

In envisioning future collaborations, we must harness the shared values embedded within both traditions. The concepts of mercy, social justice, and community resonate deeply within Christianity and Islam, offering fertile ground for collective action. Faith-based initiatives aimed at alleviating poverty, combating discrimination, and fostering peace often attract participation from both Christians and Muslims. Whether it is through joint charitable efforts or collaborative interfaith dialogues, these actions exemplify the enduring spirit of goodwill that can emerge when we focus on our commonalities rather than our differences.

We have highlighted the importance of rituals and celebrations—cultural expressions rooted in both faiths that help foster a sense of community and belonging. As Christians celebrate Christmas and Easter, Muslims observe Ramadan and Eid. These practices can serve as platforms for unity—a chance for believers to share meals, stories, and traditions that illuminate the richness of diverse practices while recognising a shared spiritual essence.

To ignite a transformative impact, education plays a pivotal role. As discussed in earlier chapters, integrating interfaith studies into academic curricula can foster environments of understanding among young people. Reflecting on personal experiences, we find that educational institutions can serve as incubators for empathy, encouraging students to explore the beliefs, histories, and practices of their peers. Investing in youth-led initiatives can empower the next generation to engage in dialogues that transcend fear and foster bridges, paving the way toward a more harmonious world.

The importance of mentorship cannot be overstated in this quest for unity. By mentoring young leaders from both faith traditions, seasoned individuals can instil values of coexistence and respect. Personal anecdotes of successful leaders illustrate how sharing stories of reconciliation and understanding can equip future generations with the tools necessary to advocate for a peaceful coexistence.

As we envision a common future, we must hold sacred the lessons learned from our shared journey. In a world increasingly marked by division and strife, both Christians and Muslims possess the power to influence broader narratives of faith and community. Recognising our intertwined journeys allows us to imagine a world where collective efforts could result in genuine interconnectedness, where diversity is celebrated as an attribute rather than a barrier.

The challenge lies in our willingness to confront the difficult conversations, engage in empathetic dialogues, and embrace the complexity of our identities. Encouraging candid reflections about our differences can ultimately reinforce our shared goals. We have witnessed individuals share their experiences of resilience and forgiveness, reminding us that reconciliation is possible through mutual understanding.

As we conclude this journey through the intertwined narratives of Christianity and Islam, let us embrace the call to unity. Words have the power to shape perceptions; thus, when we speak of our faiths, we must do so with the intent to uplift rather than alienate. Engaging in practices that emphasise common ground while respecting differences can inspire us to act for the greater good.

In closing, we stand at a precipice—an opportunity to shape the future as we navigate our shared humanity. The vision of a world in which Christians and Muslims collaborate for the sake of peace not only resonates through history but calls us into action today. It is in this spirit of unity that we must continue to weave our stories together.

As we apply the lessons learned from this book to our lives, let us challenge ourselves to step beyond our comfort zones and seek dialogue with those who hold different beliefs. Together, we can build a legacy grounded in understanding—one that acknowledges the threads of our shared journey. As we walk forward, let us create new narratives that honour our shared heritage, foster hope, and encourage cooperation, laying the foundation for a future enriched by diverse faiths and united in purpose.

This book, "Faiths Entwined," reminds us that while our journeys may be distinct, we are drawn toward the same light—a divine call toward love, peace, and transcendent shared values.

A Call to Unity

In a world marked by diversity, the tapestry of humanity presents a unique blend of cultures, beliefs, and traditions that hold within them the potential for misunderstanding, conflict, and also profound unity. As the pages of history unfold, the narratives of individuals and communities reveal a shared longing for connection, acceptance, and harmony. In this spirit, we extend a heartfelt call to unity—an appeal for individuals from different faiths, backgrounds, and walks of life to come together in dialogue, empathy, and partnership.

The current climate in our global society often highlights divisions—ranging from political ideologies to religious beliefs—that may foster animosity and fear. Yet, beneath these layers of discord lies a steadfast truth: our shared humanity. We all harbour dreams, desires, fears, and joys that connect us across barriers and borders. Just as threads in a tapestry contribute to its beauty and strength, our varied faiths and experiences enrich our collective existence. By embracing the idea of unity, we can transform our differences into instruments that foster compassion, collaboration, and understanding.

The foundation of this call to unity is the recognition that dialogue is essential. It encourages a space where ideas can be exchanged openly, where stories can be shared candidly, and where hearts can connect. Interfaith dialogue invites us to listen—to hear the voices of those who may have lived experiences vastly different from our own. These conversations fill the gaps of misunderstanding and illuminate the common ground that often lies obscured by preconceived notions.

In inviting diverse voices to the table, we create opportunities for mutual respect and recognition. When individuals from Christianity and Islam, alongside other faiths, share their beliefs, stories, and practices, they enrich one another's understanding. Such interactions can debunk myths, dispel stereotypes, and foster realistic portrayals of differing perspectives. By humanising each other's narratives, we cultivate empathy and dismantle the walls of division.

Take, for instance, an initiative launched in a community where Christians and Muslims gathered to share their beliefs during Ramadan and Lent. Each group offered reflections on their practices, and the sacred significance of fasting turned into a shared experience of sacrifice and contemplation. In witnessing one another's customs, a profound respect was forged. Community members began to appreciate the intention behind these rituals and how they resonate deeply with both faiths' call to serve humanity. These moments of recognition and understanding can ripple outwards, creating pathways for continued engagement and commitment to community well-being.

Moreover, education plays a pivotal role in fostering a culture of unity. Including teachings on interfaith collaboration and dialogue in educational curriculums can inspire younger generations to carry the torch of understanding. Children who learn about the beauty of diversity in culture and faith are likely to become adults who advocate for inclusion and respect. Imagine classrooms where stories of shared beliefs, mutual respect, and collaborative endeavours are not exceptions but the norms. Such educational initiatives would sow seeds of compassion and empower children to recognise the inherent dignity in every individual.

Communities that prioritise education can also develop programs for adults, where workshops and seminars bring together individuals from various faiths. These gatherings can focus on communal narratives of love, compassion, and service, thereby reinforcing the importance of solidarity in addressing social issues such as poverty, injustice, and environmental degradation. Engaging diverse faith communities around such causes would undoubtedly demonstrate the unity of purpose that transcends religious doctrines and inspires collective action.

As we explore pathways to unity, it is crucial to remember that the efficacy of dialogue and education needs to be complemented by individual responsibility. Each one of us bears a role in fostering understanding within our spheres of influence—whether it be at work, in our neighbourhoods, or within our families. When we approach conversations with an open heart and a willingness to listen, we contribute to a ripple effect of respect and empathy. Simple acts of kindness can break down barriers and create bridges of connection. When we choose to see one another not as representatives of our faiths but as fellow human beings sharing this planet, we elevate the conversation beyond religious differences.

Furthermore, we must also engage in acts of community service, as these endeavours not only contribute to the greater good but also create opportunities to work side by side, cultivating friendships and a sense of unity among diverse groups. Interfaith service events can be impactful, as they allow individuals to channel their faith into action, driven by shared values of compassion and charity. Whether organising food drives, working at shelters, or participating in community clean-up efforts, these collaborative actions underline our common commitment to improving our world.

In such initiatives, it is the stories shared and the connections formed that become the heartbeat of unity. Members of one faith community may find themselves inspired by the dedication of those from another faith, realising that their shared mission to serve mirrors the heartfelt teachings from their sacred texts. These experiences can transform understanding into friendships, often resulting in collaborative movements aimed at addressing societal challenges together.

Christianity and Islam - Two paths, One Purpose

As we extend this call to unity, we must acknowledge the barrier of apathy that often stifles meaningful engagement. We live in a time where distractions abound, and confronting our biases demands patience and courage. However, the pursuit of unity requires intentionality; it is about committing to reaching out rather than retreating into comfort zones. Reaching across divides can be challenging, but it is essential to recognise that growth often lies at the edge of discomfort.

This commitment can be nurtured through the example of leaders in both Christianity and Islam who advocate for peace and interfaith initiatives. Their engagement serves as a beacon of hope and inspiration for followers, reinforcing the belief that unity can be achieved. As we hear their voices calling for collaboration, we can reflect on our roles as individuals—the ways we can actively promote unity in action, whether through social media, community groups, or simple conversations with friends and family.

Additionally, embracing cultural exchange can amplify our pathways toward unity. The arts, including music, literature, and visual expressions, are powerful vehicles for conveying the complexities of faith and culture. Collaborative artistic endeavours that showcase the stories of both religions can foster understanding while celebrating the beauty of diversity. Consider projects that bring together musicians from both traditions to create multi-faceted performances that highlight shared themes of love, peace, and hope. These movements remind us that despite our differing beliefs, we are enriched by the beauty that emanates from collaboration.

As we embark on this journey toward unity, it is instrumental to recognise the power of shared narratives as foundational elements in our bonds. By recalling instances of reconciliation and friendship between faiths, we lay the groundwork for future relationships. Each tale of kindness, empathy, and respect builds trust, facilitating environments where deeper discussions can occur.

Storytelling not only preserves the journey of those seeking unity but also provides lessons for future interactions among diverse communities. These narratives can be integrated into community gatherings, learning circles, or interfaith workshops, illustrating lived experiences that inspire others to seek collaborative paths of understanding. Let us encourage young and old alike to share their experiences and listen to others with the intention that every voice matters and contributes to the larger narrative of humanity.

In conclusion, this call to unity invites individuals from all walks of life to embark on a shared journey toward understanding and acceptance. The task ahead may seem daunting, but each step taken collectively can light the way forward. Be it through dialogues, education, service, or stories shared, every action taken feeds into the greater narrative of a united humanity.

As we move forward, let us hold fast to the belief that through our differences, we can discover profound commonalities that uplift rather than divide. As advocates for peace, we are not merely seeking to coexist; we strive for collaboration, creating a legacy of understanding that endures for generations to come. Together, let us weave this vision of unity into the fabric of our communities, fostering a world where respect reigns, empathy thrives, and humanity flourishes.

We are called upon not only to envision this world but also to take action toward realising it. May we step into our roles as builders of bridges, cultivators of compassion, and champions of understanding. Let our stories intertwine and our friendships blossom, as we work tirelessly to embody the principle that respect, love, and understanding transcend the barriers of faith. Together, let us cultivate a legacy of unity that honours the richness of our diverse traditions and celebrates our shared journey as one humanity—many threads, woven together.

Daniel Meguille – Author Biography

Born in 1962 in Mikiri, a small village in Northern Cameroon, Daniel Meguille is a qualified accountant, educator, and businessman with a lifelong passion for faith, learning, and service. His early education took place at Zilve, Mora, Koza, and Dogba Primary Schools, followed by studies at Collège Adventiste de Bergström and Lycée Moderne de Maroua. He later graduated from the University of Yaoundé's Faculty of Economic Sciences and further specialised in Health and Social Care.

Daniel began his professional career as a mathematics teacher at the Adventist College of Yaoundé. He later served as Financial Manager at both the Adventist Printing Press (*Imprimerie Adventiste*) and Koza Hospital in Northern Cameroon. His expertise in financial stewardship led to his appointment as Associate Treasurer for the Central Africa Union of Seventh-day Adventist Churches.

After immigrating to the United Kingdom in 1995, Daniel continued his impactful journey through various roles in financial and community development. He worked as a business consultant specialising in start-ups with the Haringey Business Development Agency Limited, where he served as Deputy Chief Executive and later as Acting Chief Executive. During this time, he built a long-standing and trusted working relationship with the Somali community in North London. He eventually established his own business, continuing his dedication to entrepreneurship and social impact.

The son of the late Pastor Soyam Silas, Daniel carries forward his father's legacy of faith and leadership. Now based in London, he serves as an Elder at the Tottenham Seventh-day Adventist Church and remains actively engaged in business and community service.

This book project has been supported wholeheartedly by his beloved wife, Dr. Audrey Meguille Soyam, his daughters, Victoria Meguille-Soyam and Angel Meguille-Soyam, and his sons, Daniel Meguille-Soyam and Mathew Meguille-Soyam.

Christianity and Islam: Two Paths, One Purpose is a testament to Daniel Meguille's enduring commitment to fostering mutual understanding, promoting peace, and highlighting the shared spiritual values that unite humanity

www.ingramcontent.com/pod-product-compliance
Lightning Source LLC
Chambersburg PA
CBHW052029070526
44584CB00016B/1960